13 TIMELY
Fatherhood
THE ROLE OF A LIFETIME

13 TIMELESS LESSONS

Fatherhood

THE ROLE OF A LIFETIME

Paul D. Williams

Copyright © 2023 by Paul D. Williams

All rights reserved, including the right to reproduce this book, or portions thereof, in any form. No part of this book may be used or reproduced in any manner whatsoever without written permission from the publisher, except in the case of brief quotations embodied in critical articles and reviews. The views expressed herein are the responsibility of the author and do not necessarily represent the position of the publisher. For information or permission, visit authorpauldwilliams.com.

This is a work of creative nonfiction. The events herein are portrayed to the best of the author's memory. While all the stories in this book are true, some names and identifying details may have been changed to protect the privacy of the people involved.

This material is neither made, provided, approved, nor endorsed by Intellectual Reserve, Inc. or The Church of Jesus Christ of Latter-day Saints. Any content or opinions expressed, implied or included in or with the material are solely those of the owner and not those of Intellectual Reserve, Inc. or The Church of Jesus Christ of Latter-day Saints.

Cover design by MiblArt
Interior print design and layout by Sydnee Hyer
Ebook design and layout by Sydnee Hyer

WATERFIELD HOUSE

Published by Waterfield House

Paperback 979-8-9875829-0-9
Hardback 979-8-9875829-1-6
eBook 979-8-9875829-2-3

*For my dad, Duane Williams,
the greatest man I have ever known*

Noble fatherhood gives us a glimpse of the divine.

—James E. Faust

Table of Contents

Preface		xi
Acknowledgments		xv
Introduction: Welcome to Amateur Night		1
1	Poplar Grove	
	Lessons on Patriarchs	9
2	Grandma Leda	
	Lessons on Faith	23
3	*Perry Mason*, Chocolate Stars, and the Perpetual Quilt	
	Lessons on Love	37
4	Florence and Howard; Eva and Dick	
	Lessons on Knowledge	51
5	Four Widows and a Blue Ford Falcon	
	Lessons on Service	61
6	The Red Sox, the Yankees, and Dad's Back Lawn	
	Lessons on Priorities	77
7	The Journey Is the Destination	
	Lessons on Gratitude	91
8	City Beautiful	
	Lessons on Adversity	101
9	Say Uncle	
	Lessons on Living	111

10	The Best Cheeseburger in the World	
	Lessons on Worth	123
11	Believe	
	Lessons on Work	135
12	My Very Own Greek Wedding	
	Lessons on Contribution	151
13	The Windermere	
	Lessons on Discipleship	165
Notes		179
Note to the Reader		187
About the Author		189

Preface

In August of 2020, my dad's last sibling, my Uncle Burnell, passed away. My dad was the fifth of six children; two older brothers, Neldon and Bert, both World War II veterans, two older sisters, Grace and a baby who passed away the day she was born, and his younger brother Burnell. As my Uncle Burnell began to face what would be his last few weeks of mortality, my dad began to feel the loneliness of being the "last one left." He and his brother, both much younger than their older siblings, had always been close. They had shared a bedroom, date money, and life's experiences and the pending separation weighed heavy. Having lost my mom only two years before, Dad was experiencing the loss of many from his generation.

And yet my dad just kept going. After my mom passed away, he kept living; he cooked, cleaned, bought new Christmas decorations, and kept us close. Once a month he would gather us for "Family Night" and when COVID hit, he simply moved to Zoom. As he continued every family tradition and holiday, he kept things level for my siblings, myself, and our families. He remained the constant he had always been. His temple service and attention to others continued unwaveringly and he kept an extra overcoat in the back of his car—just in case he came across someone homeless who needed warmth. That warmth was one of his greatest traits as everyone he encountered, felt his love and genuine concern.

Six months after his brother's passing, my dad called me and said he felt like he should find the grave of his sister, Violet Agnes Williams. Born on November 23, 1923, Violet lived for only a few hours. When my grandparents could not afford a headstone, they did the best they could and, with heavy hearts, buried Violet in an unmarked grave in Price, Utah. With one phone call, our quest of "finding Violet" began. I called the Price Cemetery who researched the many records of infant deaths in the 1920s and finally helped me locate where she was. A few weeks later, in April of 2021, my siblings and I drove to Price with Dad and, with the help of a map, walked right to Violet's resting place. As I watched him stare at the small plot of ground, the look on his face made me wonder if he had just competed the last item the Lord had for him to do. The Williams Family had always shared a closeness quite unusual for an extended family and he had felt an urgency to find Violet. We left the cemetery, drove to a local monument business, and began the process of ordering a headstone for the aunt we had never known. Violet had been found.

Less than six weeks after gazing upon Violet's grave, my fit-as-a-fiddle, 88-year-old dad suffered a ruptured aorta that blessed him with an immediate trip through the veil, greeted no doubt by Violet, my Mom, and the rest of his loving family. For my siblings and I, the time had come for us to forge on without our earthly parents. Over the past year, I have spent a great deal of time thinking about my dad and the legacy he left. While he did not possess vast worldly wealth, he left a storehouse of memories and experiences that continue to strengthen our families. His life pursuits were never focused on his career or material possessions. My father's energies and time were devoted to the Lord and to his family. Despite serving in the church throughout his life, he never missed a ball game, a concert, a performance, a play, or a vacation that involved his children and grandchildren. We never doubted his priorities. His was a perspective of what mattered most and those whom he served and interacted with never doubted his sincere love for them and interest in them. The legacy he built for us and the lessons we learned from him carry us to this day.

When I became a father, my goal was to do what my own father had done and what his father, and his father, and his father had done. Each one had built and left a legacy that was strong enough for their descendants to stand upon. I thought—if I can come close to doing the same—I would leave a meaningful contribution that would go beyond this life. Because, as my dad always taught, the best focus was the one that looked beyond this life and into the eternities.

Such was the inspiration for this book—a collection of lessons with messages rich enough to help us see beyond what the world tries to offer. Thankfully, I had the chance to share many of these chapters with my dad before he left. And while the world today is vastly different and more challenging than the one I or my father and grandfathers lived in, messages that focus on the importance of love, the value of work, and the worth of a soul do not change from generation to generation. Character has always mattered, and it always will because that is what truly builds and defines the individual and shapes and changes the world.

When I consider with earthly eyes how different the world of today is from the one I grew up in, it can be intimidating. The pace of change comes so fast and furiously and the distances between generational change seem to be shrinking. Even the short gap of five years between our third and fourth children created different issues and challenges in raising what we have often referred to as our first batch of children and our second. The effects of cell phones, video games, pornography, and shifting opinions on morality and sexuality can appear daunting. And yet the basics of human nature are the same and the hopes and excitement of youth continue from one generation to the next. We understand more than we think and the guidance of the Lord who does know all is the greatest assurance of all. We are up to the task of fatherhood.

It is also important to understand that having a loving, engaged father of our own is not a pre-requisite to our being one. We all come to this life with a character and strength designed to enable us to overcome rough starts. Each of us can access that power through prayer to know how to bless our children's lives.

The void of my parents will never be filled until I see them again. However, their legacy lives on because of what they taught, what they focused on, and how they lived. Theirs truly was the richer, fuller, deeper life with joyous memories that bring a smile to my face each day.

On a recent Sunday, during a lesson on being Christlike, I opened my scriptures to a page where I had placed my dad's funeral program. There, staring at me from the pages, was his picture. Taken in the latter years of his life, his face wore the soft, kind smile it always had, the love in his eyes, and the wisdom borne of a lifetime of service. His face glowed with what Alma referred to as having "the image of God engraven upon" his countenance. It was a very familiar look for he always wore the banner of discipleship. Completely devoted to the Lord and to his family, he was a master of knowing and living what mattered most. My great hope is that, in some future day, my children will be able to say the same of me.

Acknowledgments

Journaling my thoughts on fatherhood, making notes, and even giving talks on the subject is nothing like weaving those same stories into a book. The journey of collecting these experiences was long. Trying to compile meaningful lessons and valuable tales of fatherhood into a succinct collection to both keep the readers' attention and bless their lives is both daunting and humbling, and I have many people to thank for getting me this far.

First and foremost, I wish to thank my wonderful wife JoAnn. She is a woman of remarkable strength. Her faith and confidence in me never wavered. She has a great eye for editing, and she has spent hours reading and re-reading the chapters of this book. Through it all, her positive feedback motivated me to finish. She is the greatest source of strength in my life and the best thing that ever happened to me.

Second, I wish to thank all seven of my incredible children. They amaze me every day, and I could not be more grateful for their love and patience. They inspire me to be better, and I never imagined how much joy they would bring to my life. The love I have for and within my family is a blessing beyond anything I could have imagined.

Next, I wish to thank my parents, Duane and Maxine Williams. My father—a powerfully spiritual man with an eternal perspective in a small frame—and my mother—who lifted and built people up with her incredible heart and her out-of-left-field sense of humor all through her life—together built a home of love and joy that is incomprehensible. They filled the reservoir of my mind with memories that will always bless me.

And then there are the many other people who have inspired me throughout my life. My in-laws, uncles and aunts, grandparents, friends, professional acquaintances, and others have provided examples of determination, love, sacrifice, and contribution that have made me a better person.

And last, but certainly not least, the incredible editing team at Eschler Editing for their work, support, and advice. To Michael and Trina, who encouraged me and brought me back from "memory lane" when it was necessary; to Lindsay, whose patience and support always encouraged me; to Brittany for her copyedits (Brittany, how do you do that voodoo you do so well?); to Angela, whose view from thirty thousand feet kept me focused on my purpose and audience; and to Michele and AJ, who helped along the publishing path. They are a talented group of people.

Fatherhood has been the role of a lifetime for me. I invite all fathers to learn as much as they can, work hard, pray harder, and most of all, enjoy it.

> *"To put the world in order, we must first put the nation in order; to put the nation in order, we must first put the family in order; to put the family in order, we must first cultivate our personal life; we must first set our hearts right."*
>
> —Confucius

INTRODUCTION

Welcome to Amateur Night

"Call off your dogs."

Snow blanketed the Salt Lake Valley. My lifelong home never ceased to capture my imagination with its picturesque winter wonderland scenes and frosty windows. My life changed forever on a January day, complete with a clear blue sky, the bright sun glistening, and deep, untouched snow.

My wife, JoAnn, and I had married nearly five years prior. We made plans for our future and expected, among other things, to begin our family. Our new life together came along nicely. JoAnn graduated from college a few years after me, and together we pursued the American Dream in the workforce. We both progressed in our professions and traveled often. We built a new home, snuck away for long weekends out of town, and shopped and dined whenever the fever struck. Life was wonderful with one exception—no children. We waited, wondered, prayed, and did all the things people do when they earnestly desire something.

As the weeks turned into months and then years, our disappointment grew. Why was such a seemingly worthwhile desire eluding us? Despite the joys we experienced, our new home was too quiet, and the backseat of our car was too empty. We ached for children. Doctors suggested it may not happen; we prayed harder. We sought operations to cure JoAnn's endometriosis.

On one frustrating night, we called our bishop and asked for a blessing for JoAnn. He came over, laid his hands on her head, and blessed her. When he concluded his prayer with an "amen," somehow, I knew the wait was over. It was a powerful feeling.

Within a month, on one magical, miraculous day, JoAnn discovered she was pregnant.

Several weeks later the news got even better—she was expecting twins.

Like every excited set of parents, we prepared for every seeming need. We filled our days with preparations for the babies. We bought all the baby things we had always been afraid to buy and told anyone who would listen that we were having twins. JoAnn joined groups for mothers of twins, and we built a nursery for two. When I found out she was having two boys, I immediately began looking at baseball, Lincoln Logs, and having my lawn mowed with an entirely new set of expectations.

The most wonderful joy was watching JoAnn. The woman who granted me my dreams was finally getting her dream fulfilled. She was going to be a mother.

As the time approached, we enrolled in birthing classes. I struggled to adapt to that adventure. My excitement to be a father and desire to serve JoAnn did not include a desire to be personally involved in the delivery. It was she who had experienced all the discomforts of pregnancy, and I felt no amount of simulated sympathy would help. I did enjoy consuming an increased amount of pizza when she went on bed rest, but that was hardly a sacrifice.

So, at the appointed hour, I checked her into the hospital, sat by her side, and held her hand.

After hours of labor and with the inevitable approaching, they moved JoAnn into an operating room to be prepared due to the higher risk to her and the twins. A team that numbered in the double digits—doctors, nurses, and a group of observing residency students—as well as every available piece of equipment except the kitchen sink waited for us there. It looked like a sellout. I staggered into the room behind JoAnn and into the vast unknown.

As her labor and fatigue, along with my anxiety, mounted, the moment finally arrived. In what looked like a circus act, one doctor delivered the first baby while another one pushed on JoAnn's stomach to keep the second in a head-first position.

At 2:17 a.m. with barely a whimper, Williams Baby Boy A entered mortality. I held my first son in that dimly lit operating room and whispered salutations to him. He was content, wrapped tightly in a soft, warm blanket. His gaze never wavered from my face. I don't recall our conversation, but JoAnn later said, "You conversed with him as if you had known him forever." Looking into his eyes, I knew she was right.

Our solitude broke when his less content brother, Williams Baby Boy B, came screaming into mortality. For a moment I thought someone had been shot in the adjoining room. He was as beautiful as Baby Boy A, but that's where all similarities ended.

As the sellout crowd wandered out of the delivery room, JoAnn went to her room to rest, Baby Boy A went to the nursery, Baby Boy B was escorted by the nurse to the ICU for a few hours of monitored breathing, and I went to the cafeteria for a pastry.

After the excitement of delivery, our stay in the hospital over the next few days was one of ease. JoAnn was fed and taken care of; I came and went with no responsibility beyond that of presenting my insurance card to the hospital finance office; and, best of all, Baby Boys A and B were attended to by wonderful nurses, who let us sleep as often as we wanted.

Whenever the itch struck, I wandered over to the nursery, checked them out with the nurse, and rolled them down the hall to JoAnn's room where we played with them, kissed them, and showed them off to anyone who entered our small domain.

JoAnn fed them, and then off they went back to the nursery so JoAnn could rest and I could catch the 10:30 p.m. episode of *Perry Mason* on television. *Perry Mason* and pastries—I could do this fatherhood thing.

The last day of our hospital stay came with a cold slap of reality. Not the kind that occurs when you pay rent for the first time or when college begins. I'm talking about the sheer, terrifying panic that came from realizing that I had absolutely no idea what I was doing.

The overly enthusiastic nurse handed each JoAnn and me a baby and then wheeled JoAnn to the lobby. We were actually leaving. I wasn't sure what was happening. No more nurses, no more help. What would become of my *Perry Mason* and pastries?

The nurse loaded the boys into the car, making a show of how to make sure they were strapped in. Next, JoAnn traded her wheelchair for a passenger seat. It was up to me to take the wheel. I stood by the car, dazed and frozen. The nurse seemed amused. She smiled and said, "Good luck." I think she chuckled all the way back into the hospital.

I climbed into the car. Is it possible to be excited and numb at the same time? I turned the key and drove our new family home.

The garage seemed smaller. I maneuvered our new little responsibilities out of the car, up the aisle, and into the family room. I carefully propped their car seats safely against the sofa before returning to help JoAnn in and get settled.

It was evening now. I quietly walked back into the family room, and all four of the twins' eyes arrested my attention. Our first staring contest. I stood squarely in front of them and stared. They stared back. I knew they were innocent and so trusting. They had just left the presence of God. But they seemed to be saying, "Now, what are you going to do with us?"

Smiling nervously, I knew if anyone were watching me, I would fail to disguise the fact that I had no idea what I was doing. I thought,

"Welcome to amateur night." Far in the distant corner of my mind, I heard the unmistakable sound of a snare drum and cymbal.

I felt unprepared. How much time, study, and work went into being a professional? Doctors go to school for years before actually practicing medicine. Attorneys and college professors obtain advanced graduate degrees before they're let loose into the world. Success in any pursuit doesn't come overnight. Hours, months, and years of hard work and experience are required for achievement and great responsibility.

And then there was me. A new father, with two humans staring at me, with absolutely no training to handle it—amateur night indeed.

The only requirement for me to obtain Matthew's and Johnathan's custody was demonstrating I had a matching wristband. That was it. There was no exam, no proof of diploma or certification, no oath to take. I was their father, and they were my children. The realization hit me like a sledgehammer. The greatest responsibility in the world, and I had no idea what to do next. Have you experienced that feeling yet?

I guess most fathers feel their lives and priorities change the moment they hold their first child. Actor Mark Wahlberg stated, "This is my most important role. If I fail at this, I fail at everything."[1] Fathers desire to succeed. That is our common ground. But our successes and failures come gradually as we compile a memory bank of lessons, mistakes, and a heap of diapers.

There is no shortage of ideas on how to be a father. The world offers catalogs of lessons through social media, theological and doctrinal studies, and self-proclaimed experts. Yet, some of the best sources for learning come from a desire to learn on the job. Even if you feel, like I did, that you are in uncharted waters, know that there are compasses, maps, and sextons at your disposal if you know where to look for them.

The world is influenced by individuals of stature, wealth, and academic accomplishment. We think they've "made it," so they must know better than the rest of us. Books have been written by experts in parenting, childcare, and psychology with the assumption that their scholarly attainment gives them a leg up. Other self-help books depict fathers with great achievements, which leads to the conclusion that success in one area must guarantee success in all others.

While insight is always helpful, these types of manuscripts miss the spot where the proverbial rubber meets the proverbial road. They lack in the practical.

I'm not trained as a certified expert, nor do I believe that the only fathers worth writing about are the famous ones. This book is written by an everyday dad, for everyday dads. Unseen fathers around the world go about doing great things every day, one child at a time, and never tell their story. It's easy to feel like our experience is worthless to share. I've felt that way.

That, however, is not the way our Father sees it. He constantly taught about "the one." Consider the parables The Lord taught—the lost sheep, the prodigal son, the woman brought to Him in sin. Those parables focused on the one. Translation: You matter. Your efforts matter. And we each have a story worth sharing.

One of the greatest gifts we all possess is an innate ability and understanding that often seems to come from deep inside. This spiritual gift was given to us to aid us on our mission in mortality. And if you believe you have a specific mission, doesn't it make sense that you came prepackaged to accomplish it? Naturally, you are not alone.

Even if you feel alone. Don't forget you also have the examples of the Divine to guide us as fathers. Jesus Christ came into the world and, through His ministry, set the example as to how we should conduct ourselves in any circumstance. In 3 Nephi 27:27, The Savior instructed His newly called disciples in how to manage their responsibilities as judges when He said, "Therefore, what manner of men ought ye to be? Verily I say unto you, even as I am." That powerful, short sermon from the Master speaks volumes to those millions who seek to lead their families.

It also fits the definition of what Thomas S. Monson, former President of The Church of Jesus Christ of Latter-day Saints, called "the clarion call."[2]

In my life, like yours, many fathers blazed the trail before me, preparing me for the role I now play. For me, this included my own father. His life marked a standard of goodness I want to achieve. And while not every man has that kind of example, each of us has men and women in our lives who influence us for good and leave lasting imprints upon us.

As I have observed the stories of so many, I'm continually amazed by the constant stream of people who overcome difficult beginnings. Regardless of our own diverse beginnings, wandering paths, and varied strengths, each father can become the best in his field.

Throughout my tenure as a father, I have succeeded, and I have failed; I have had great days and I have had bad days. And yet I am just like you: I love my children more than I could ever comprehend, and I seek to be a better father each day. Success as a father is defined one child at a time and one day at a time. Our hopes and dreams are tied to them, and our greatest goals are to raise them to be good people, good neighbors, good citizens, and loving children of God. We know each child has their agency, and we cannot control what they do. We can, however, work to give our absolute best efforts as we endeavor to help them and build them up.

On that perfect January day when I brought newborn twins home, I didn't realize we would be blessed with five more children. When JoAnn miraculously became pregnant with our seventh child, I called our old bishop and said the first thing that came to my mind: "Hey Bishop, call off your dogs."

Williams Baby Boys A and B were the beginning of a wonderful journey, and today our home is loud with laughter and love and our backseat is full of children. Now, after our long wait, each child—their happiness and their exaltation—are my greatest dreams and my greatest work. And they are also my greatest joy as nothing has brought me more happiness than being a husband and father.

Throughout my imperfect journey, I have both intentionally learned and stumbled upon lessons of fatherhood that have enhanced my life and made me better. These countless moments and wonderful experiences have filled my life with joy and created memories that transcend any individual success I've enjoyed.

My journey has been thrilling, with highs and lows; however, is that not what life is all about? The secret lies in discovery: the discovery of life viewed through the eyes of each child and the discovery of what matters most.

It is my humble belief that we as fathers are engaged in the greatest responsibility and the highest honor that could ever be bestowed upon us. Will we be perfect? Not even close. But we can strive for it. The legendary Hall of Fame football coach, Vince Lombardi wrapped it up perfectly. Said Lombardi, "Perfection is not attainable. But if we chase perfection, we can catch excellence."[3]

Keep going and give fatherhood all you have within you. You are enough. Your efforts matter. And never forget to enjoy the ride.

I

Poplar Grove

Lessons on Patriarchs

"Do you think they're serving coleslaw?"

I imagine there were clear blue skies on a day well over five thousand years ago during one of the earth's greatest family reunions ever held. The place was the lush, green, beautiful valley of Adam-ondi-Ahman, where Adam gathered his posterity together for one last time. History is light on the details. We do not have a date. Although if you do the math based on the book of Genesis, it looks to be approximately 3,073 years before the birth of Christ. Further, we don't know what food they served or whether they had a name-your-great-uncle contest. However, this particular gathering had great significance to Adam and Eve and their family. Father Adam knew his time left on earth was short, and he intended to give one last blessing to those he loved.

These were the days of extended mortality, and among the likely righteous posterity who gathered would have been Adam's steady eight-hundred-year-old son, Seth, so much like his father except for the difference in their ages. Also present would have been Adam's great-great-great-great-grandson, a 308-year-old spiritual giant named Enoch.

Not quite middle-aged by the standards of the day, Enoch was a man of great strength who had already established his city of Zion that was a mere 125 years away from being translated. Adam's sixth great-grandson Lamech, another likely attendee, was still a youngster at the age of fifty-six who had not yet seen the arrival of a particular son who would go on to make a name for himself by building an ark, of all the things. What a span of years. Attending this family party would be akin to walking into a modern-day reunion only to overhear your fourteenth great-uncle, Christopher Columbus, at the table next to you asking his wife, "Do you think they're serving coleslaw?"

However, this was no ordinary family, and this reunion was to be no ordinary reunion. This was to be a great experience in history as Adam was joined by the great high priests of the age from the second generation of his family down to the eighth.

At 927 years old, Adam was still three years away from his death; however, he had no doubt lived a dozen lifetimes of experiences. I have always thought if Adam had not seen it all, nobody has. In what must be one of the great understatements of holy writ, Doctrine and Covenants 107:56 reads that Adam was "bowed down with age." And yet here he was, gathering everyone together for a celebration of celebrations.

He and Eve had literally started with nothing. When they left the Garden of Eden to "make their own way," there was not a sea of sparkler-waving family and friends or a van being crammed full of gifts by the best man and his cohorts. Likewise, there was no honeymoon, nor was there a mattress and box springs set from the in-laws. They departed into the land rush of land rushes—no competition and acres as far as the eye could see. They were not only making their own way: they were making everything along the way. Everything they did was a first, and everything they acquired came as a direct result of their own hands, hard work, and ingenuity.

Is it surprising to consider that the first man and first woman who had talked and walked with God during their sojourn in the Garden of

Eden would have children in the first generation who would be rebellious non-believers? And yet this was the lot of Adam and Eve. They endured illness, hardship, and heartbreak without the advice and reassurance of earthly parents. Amid all of this, they suffered the ultimate sorrow when their son, Cain, murdered his own brother, Abel.

However, through their long time together, they no doubt experienced great joy with children, multiple generations of grandchildren, and developments that advanced the quality of life for their posterity. Now, under those likely blue skies of Adam-ondi-Ahman, it was time for one last blessing from the great patriarch.

The prophet Joseph Smith taught that Adam desired to bless his posterity because "he wanted to bring them into the presence of God."[4] Over 140 years later, another modern-day prophet, Ezra Taft Benson, taught, "Adam and his descendants entered into the priesthood order of God. Today we would say they went to the House of the Lord and received their blessings."[5]

When we consider Joseph Smith's words, that Adam wanted his posterity to be brought "into the presence of God," it is hard to imagine that his last words of love and encouragement would have been to play harder, spend more time at the proverbial office or in the fields, or to create wealth so that their families would be taken care of financially. To a man of Adam's age and wisdom, those things would most likely seem completely insignificant. Adam's last message was, no doubt, a powerful sermon on what really mattered: our relationship with God, our relationship with our family, and the obedience that enables us to be brought "into the presence of God." Surely it was a great spiritual event, for at the conclusion of his blessing, "the Lord appeared unto them, and they rose up and blessed Adam, and called him Michael, the prince, the archangel. And the Lord administered comfort unto Adam, and said unto him: I have set thee to be at the head; a multitude of nations shall come of thee, and thou art a prince over them forever" (Doctrine and Covenants 107:54–55).

Adam, father and grandfather to all living people, knew his days were coming to an end. Before that day came, he had one last message that he wanted them to hear, one last note of encouragement and love. With death near at hand and with a perspective and wisdom sown of over nine hundred years of experience, Adam needed to share what mattered most.

Understanding what matters most comes to us all at one point or another. We have experienced moments of fear, doubt, or difficulty when the suddenness of mortality shows itself and our minds quickly put aside things that are fleeting for the things that matter.

One of those times occurred for me when our seventh child was born. We had not anticipated any problems, and JoAnn's childbirth appeared to be routine. However, when our baby boy had difficulty breathing from the onset, they took him for X-rays and identified a diaphragmatic hernia, a hole in his diaphragm that had allowed some of his internal organs to move into his chest. Hours seemingly became days as we stood helplessly by during his examination and transfer to Primary Children's Hospital.

Unsure of his future, my thoughts turned to those things of eternal significance. If I had one last message to give my son, or any of my children, what would it be? I would desire to use God's priesthood to bless them one last time, to plead with them to keep their covenants, and to remind them to seek after those things that really matter. I would beg them to love each other and to love the Lord.

At that moment, I was given a small glimpse into the great role of a patriarch. What a blessing a worthy, faithful patriarch can be to his posterity if he honors the priesthood, stands firm in the faith, and seeks after those things that outlast this life.

The importance of a strong father has been stressed since Adam's time. His last great blessing set a standard that has been repeated throughout history and recorded throughout the scriptures, further evidence of their importance in God's eyes. Some of the greatest advice, admonitions, and warnings given have come through the utterances of aged fathers, great patriarchs who wanted to provide a last piece of instruction to their posterity. The words given to us from well-known patriarchs such as Abraham, Isaac, and Jacob from the Old Testament and Lehi, Nephi, and Alma from the Book of Mormon provide guidance and insight that have withstood the test of time. They all pointed not to the world, not to possessions, but to God and to family, and their messages have resonated throughout the ages.

In most cases, the roles of patriarch and father are the same. They love, they lead, they exhort, and they look after. Merriam-Webster defines a patriarch as "one of the scriptural fathers of the human race or of the Hebrew people" as well as "a man who is a father or founder."[6] The word itself comes from the Latin word *pater*, which means father.[7] In those definitions, we see that a father is also a leader. Of course, he does not lead alone, and his role to lead in tandem with his wife is vital to the family unit.

When we consider the leaders that we see day-to-day, we see men and women who each have their own definitions and style of leadership. These approaches range from love to brutality, encouragement to derision, census building to coercion. There is no shortage of examples and advice givers. However, when I consider the greatest leaders I've ever known—in the past or the present—they have led with two distinct characteristics. First, they have put the interests of their followers over those of their own. Second, they have conducted themselves in a way in which the vast majority of their followers wanted to follow them. I'm not referring to those with a blind, cult-like mentality; I'm referring to those who trust their leaders, respect them, and see their vision for where they want to go and how they want to get there. In short, if we want to lead out as fathers, we must do it in a way that our children will want to follow us and learn from us.

But what defines leadership? How do you develop your vision for your family when you are the leader? In my professional life, I've spent much of my career working with various businesses and organizations in strategic planning. The process of moving an organization from point A to B to C is fascinating. Entities who identify who they are, decide where they want to go, and stick to their plans most often enjoy great success. Those who lose sight of those things, those who become distracted by pursuing new ideas that take them beyond what they know how to do best, often don't find the success they are chasing.

The banking crisis of 2008 and 2009 decimated heretofore strong community banks. Many of them knew who they were but became distracted by the lure of a skyrocketing real estate market. In their zeal to take advantage of the growth, they eased up on loan policies and went into unknown geographic markets. Even after other markets began to crumble, the bankers yet unscathed believed somehow that their outcome would be different, that they would withstand the times. They were wrong. For the most part, the banks who remained standing were those who stuck with what they knew and stayed on the path they knew. While they also suffered losses, their planning and focus enabled them to survive.

Who is your family? Where do you want your family to go? And how will you stick to your plan to achieve it? We must know—and never lose sight of—who we are and where we want to go. Further, we must focus our efforts so the distractions of work, hobbies, and the enticements of the world, both good and evil, do not sway us from the great potential and blessings that wait for us. Every decision you make and every goal you set should align with a clear mission statement.

We must never expect perfection. The pattern is all throughout the scriptures, or in other words, the teachings from the greatest leader the world has ever seen, Jesus Christ. In His sermons we learn the importance of love, faith, tolerance, service, and so many other attributes. When we take our own journey and align our hopes and priorities with His, we are ready to lead, for a leader cannot take someone on a journey that they themselves have never made. The experiences, hardships, and lessons of our lives are part of our journey that prepares us to lead our children on theirs. To start, we must set our lives and our houses in order.

In my early years, my family lived in a cottage-style home set among the quiet, tree-lined streets of a west-side Salt Lake City neighborhood known as Poplar Grove. To a small boy, it was a world unto itself. We knew we could depend on the corner grocer, who knew our names. We frequented the walk-up hamburger joint across the street, and the shaving cream and conversation flowed equally at the neighborhood barber shop. Right in the middle of all this stood a two-block long park surrounded on all four sides by bungalow houses with freshly mowed lawns. Poplar Grove even came complete with a small vacant lot on 900 West where Christmas trees were sold every December. Brigham Young's famous quote "This is the right place" was obviously uttered before he ever saw Poplar Grove; however, the phrase fit our neighborhood. Life there was like 1950s television complete with hand-push lawn mowers and weekly visits from the requisite slow-moving musical ice cream truck.

Our small neighborhood was safe, and each day I walked to school with my friend Gary Jensen. The mid-century Pioneer Stake Center of The Church of Jesus Christ of Latter-day Saints was just a few blocks down the street. This church house was no ordinary place of worship. It was a great gathering place, complete with two full-length chapels separated by a cavernous gymnasium and a lattice-trimmed kitchen where routine pot-luck dinners were the order of the day. This granddaddy of churches was the site of my first raffle victory—a Thanksgiving turkey—as well as my first train ride on a pint-sized, homemade version with wheels instead of rails and a few too many cars to control.

Our well-meaning conductor boarded us all and then took the first turn down the long parking lot a little too tight, promptly tipping the entire train on its side. My memory is a jumble of crying children, the sound of parents rushing in, and the chubby face of my three-year-old sister staring at me as she lay on top of me. But all was well, and our confidence in the engineer was quickly bought off by relieved parents who served us cookies by the gross. Even a five-year-old has a price.

Poplar Grove was the stuff life is made of. We did not have vast worldly wealth, but no amount of money could compensate for what we had. I had friends on Indiana Avenue, Navajo Street, 700 South, and everywhere in between. Everyone seemed to have my best interest at heart.

The Pioneer Stake, home to the Poplar Grove wards, had no shortage of distinguished alumni either, which included, among others, Thomas S. Monson and Harold B. Lee. However, most of the people there were great people doing small things in great ways, influencing and building people for good along the way.

The examples of these men and women taught me fatherhood. The good works of uncles, neighbors, leaders, colleagues, and other associates defined what it means to be a good man. Of all these men, the greatest man I have ever known also put down roots in Poplar Grove—my dad. He was the Will Rogers of my life: he never met a man he did not like. His innate qualities of tolerance, kindness, and charity touched all he served. He always sought to leave everyone better than he found them. His grasp of what really matters exceeded that of anyone I have ever known.

As the patriarch of our family, he taught us the importance of time and perspective. These lessons came quietly over many years of his practice and our observance of his intentional cadence. When he walked by, I felt light. When he spoke or gave advice, I saw his eternal perspective. Things of the world never mattered to him. The Lord, his family, and the "one"—in other words, whoever he was talking to—those were the things that mattered to him. If anything ever seemed chaotic or even out of the ordinary, I was always able to look to my dad. His reassuring, peaceful smile provided the reassurance that all was well.

His cadence of life was enhanced by its pace. While he worked hard with a sense of urgency, his pace was always steady and uncluttered. It created time: time for us, time to play ball, time to go camping, time to just be together. How is our pace today? Our entertainment, sporting, recreational, and technological options are so abundant that it almost seems overwhelming.

One of my first thoughts upon becoming a father was how much I would be able to do for my children. Vacations, piano and violin lessons, little league baseball, tennis, dance, the sky was the limit, and we would do it all. Then, I remembered my dad's pace.

We were less scheduled, we ate together, and we enjoyed simpler times together. Some of my fondest memories are of my parents loading us into their 1964 Chevy II, buying us a roll of Necco's candy wafers and a small root beer, and then driving us into downtown Salt Lake to see the lights of the city. That was it. And I loved it.

Today's world is vastly different from my early days in Poplar Grove. Each day still has the same number of hours, and as fathers and co-leaders in our homes, we may set our own pace. Of course, there are various ways to approach leadership. The best strategy I have seen for success comes from leaders and fathers who walk with their children along the way. Not far ahead or far away, but with them. This leadership style enables us to be engaged and understand the pertinent needs of our children. Best of all, it makes us participants in life's events, enabling us to share in the victories and give love and support in defeat.

The flip side of the equation is those who lead from the front, barking orders to those who may hear behind. These leaders remind me of the oft-repeated phrase "There go my people, I'd better catch up with them." The saddest tale comes from those who, distracted by other pursuits, do not lead at all, for surely the day will come when it will be too late, and they will realize just how much they have missed. Let us be among those who walk with our children.

We have much to offer in this world of ours, and much of it is good. In our well-intended efforts to give our children more than we had, we often end up busying our lives with every activity possible and whatever else seems to be trending, doing our part to fuel our consumer-driven economy by buying everything we can get our hands on. We then spend countless hours on the internet, cell phones, and video games while we wonder why our kids are texting their friends, who are sitting on the couch across from them. We long for the days of simplicity and wonder why we don't eat together and sit on the proverbial front porch, but then we distract ourselves by looking at our planning paraphernalia that is roughly the size of the Gutenberg Bible and bask in our busyness.

These pursuits are not inherently a bad thing. Indeed, we can find much joy in helping our children excel, build their talents, and enjoy entertainment and recreation together as a family. I believe, however, that we can also find magic in not overscheduling our lives. Children grow up too fast. Why not slow down the pace and find our way to those simple family activities that will give us the time to teach and build? In an era of instant everything, meaningful time with our children requires disengagement from our crowded lives and attention to time together. I soon realized that the many aspirations I had for my children, things I thought would enable them to experience the most of their childhood, would overload them, overwhelm JoAnn and me, and eliminate those simple yet wonderful impromptu barbeques and cool summer nights with lemonade on the front lawn.

In our role as patriarchs, we must guide our children through the labyrinth of choices they will be offered, both good and bad. But we can't always be with them. Life is exciting; it may also be peaceful. The ability to obtain both comes from an understanding of how the Spirit speaks to us. A great leader in the banking industry once reminded me that one of the best keys to my success would be taking a few moments each day to stare out the window and think about the most important tasks that would get me to where I needed to be. The same can be said of our efforts to teach our children to assume a pace that allows the Spirit into their lives. When we take the time to learn how to follow the Spirit, we naturally come to a formula for success.

One of my favorite scriptural references about learning how to hear the Spirit comes from 1 Kings 19, where Elijah the prophet found himself on the wrong end of a death threat from Queen Jezebel. With Jezebel ruling by the side of her husband, King Ahab, Israel became increasingly wicked and began to worship Baal. As a result, the Lord sent the prophet Elijah, who summarily sealed the heavens and fled town at the command of the Lord, leaving Israel in a prolonged drought. Finally, the Lord sent Elijah back to Samaria to end the drought. Once there, he made quick work of the drought (the rest of this story is covered in a later chapter) and, in the process, humiliated Jezebel and her troup of false prophets. Apparently, this being the final insult, Jezebel determined to rid herself of Elijah.

Forewarned by the Spirit, Elijah fled. On the move again, he found a place under a juniper tree and, completely exhausted, collapsed. After a period of time, an angel appeared to Elijah, woke him up, fed him, and directed him to Mount Horeb to receive instruction. When Elijah arrived, the Lord asked him why he had come. After offering his explanation, Elijah had this experience in 1 Kings 19:11–13.

And he said, "Go forth, and stand upon the mount before the Lord. And, behold, the Lord passed by, and a great and strong wind rent the mountains, and brake in pieces the rocks before the Lord; but the Lord was not in the wind: and after the wind an earthquake; but the Lord was not in the earthquake: and after the earthquake a fire; but the Lord was not in the fire: and after the fire a still small voice. And it was so, when Elijah heard it, that he wrapped his face in his mantle, and went out, and stood in the entering in of the cave. And, behold, there came a voice unto him, and said, What doest thou here, Elijah?"

Elijah proceeded again to express his reason for coming and then received his instruction.

This experience is a reminder of how the Lord communicates with us. If our lives are too busy to listen, if our minds are too clouded with responsibility and calendaring, if our attention is too diverted to laptops, cell phones, and headphones, when will our children ever have the time and the patience to learn to first recognize and then listen to that still, small voice? Our children will have vital decisions to make throughout their lives. With the noises of the world and all of life's options, it's imperative that they leave our protective influence with the understanding of how God speaks to them. As we teach them to pray, to study the scriptures, and be quiet and listen to the voice of the Lord, they'll develop a pattern of doing whatever is necessary to receive personal revelation. And that guidance will enable them to be on the path God has for them. That guidance from the Spirit will bring our children confidence in life and confidence before the Lord.

At the base of my dad's character was his confidence before God. Of course, it did not come overnight. It came from diligently seeking obedience to, faith in, and love for God. My dad taught us the invaluable lesson from 2 Nephi 25, verses 23 and 26: "For we labor diligently to write, to persuade our children, and also our brethren, to believe in Christ, and to be reconciled to God; for we know that it is by grace that we are saved, after all we can do. . . . And we talk of Christ, we rejoice in Christ, we preach of Christ, we prophesy of Christ, and we write according to our prophecies, that our children may know to what source they may look for a remission of their sins." I've always known my dad looked to Him for everything, and that has been the great lesson of his life as well as the one I strive to teach my children.

I think that is what Adam wanted his children to know most of all. Within three years of that grand reunion at Adam-ondi-Ahman, Father Adam, as they say, went the way of all the earth. The mark he left as the earth's first patriarch set a standard that prophets, patriarchs, and fathers have followed for thousands of years since. His life was one of building his posterity and doing all within his power to bless them, build them up, and help them return to the presence of God.

Of course, very few of God's children are called to serve in visible prophetic roles. However, each of us, if we choose the opportunity, has been called as husbands and fathers alongside our wives and mothers—each a prophet of sorts but in smaller spheres called families. And while our earthly roles come to an end, our role as patriarch will live on in eternity in the organization of the celestial kingdom. The greatest gift that the patriarchs of the past left us is their legacy of lessons—lessons that, when taught and lived, are the only way back to the presence of God.

2

Grandma Leda

Lessons on Faith

"Am I almost there?"

A few short years after the pioneers of The Church of Jesus Christ of Latter-day Saints arrived in the Salt Lake Valley in 1847, Brigham Young initiated what became a decades-long colonization effort that created new communities, spread the Church's influence, and expanded industry throughout what would become the vast Utah Territory. By the time of his passing in 1877, President Young had overseen the settlement of nearly four hundred communities in what is today Arizona, California, Colorado, Hawaii, Idaho, Nevada, Utah, and Wyoming as well as Canada and Mexico.

During the 1860s small settlements began to appear in the southeast corner of present-day Idaho. In those sagebrush-covered valleys flanked by mountains with quaking aspens and pine trees, the mainstay was agriculture as the pioneers found an area ripe for growing everything from apples to onions to hay to the infamous Idaho potato. It was in one of those small farming communities called Treasureton where a baby girl, Leda May Atkinson, was born into a family of twelve children on May

Day in 1916. Leda was small, hardworking, and fiercely independent. She was never afraid to speak her mind.

She married shortly after graduating from high school only to find later that her husband was not the prize she'd expected. The Depression loomed largely, and yet, determined to live by faith and obedience, she sent him to the proverbial showers in the same efficient manner that a baseball manager hops up the dugout steps, walks slowly to the pitcher's mound, and replaces a faltering pitcher with a lefty from the bullpen. With that done, Leda took her two young sons, moved to a small apartment in Preston, Idaho, and took a job as a waitress at the local diner. Residing in that same town was a quiet man with a shy, likable smile named John Sampson. John managed the local pool hall and, after locking up, he would saunter over to the diner for a late-night dinner.

One night Leda spied him sitting at the counter. "What does your wife think of you eating out every night?" she asked.

"I'm not married," said John.

"You don't know how lucky you are, you should keep it that way!"

John didn't take her advice. In his own quiet yet persistent way, he successfully wooed Leda and married her.

Eventually they settled into a humble, two-room home in Salt Lake's Poplar Grove neighborhood in the mid-1940s. John added rooms as their family grew to six.

By the time I was old enough to know and love Leda, she had weathered her fair share of trials. In addition to her rocky first marriage, she also lost a son in a drunk driving accident. Later, after losing her beloved John, she endured the challenges that come with advancing age. Despite the obstacles of life, Leda was always happy, full of faith, resilient, and determined.

We had not lived in Poplar Grove long before Leda became an occasional babysitter, and I felt her love for me. At some point in time, she became Grandma Leda, although I'm not sure who requested that title, me or her.

Later in my life, during a time when I was struggling with a trial of my own, I returned to my roots seeking a peace I had known there. Just as we turn for help from our heavenly home, I also sought comfort from the memories of my first earthly home and my childhood. As I drove through those memory-laden streets of Poplar Grove, I stopped and parked right in front of Grandma Leda's house. I walked up the sidewalk to her tiny front porch and knocked quietly on the screen door which fronted her wide-open front door. In a matter of seconds, this diminutive ninety-year-old woman appeared. With much of her sight diminished, she still looked at me and knew who I was.

We visited in her semi-dark living room, and I happily sat listening to the stories I'd loved as a boy as well as the events that had occurred in the intervening years. Just into her tenth decade of life she was still at it: giving cookies to the mailman, talking with the construction workers across the street, and haggling over the cost to repair a water heater. We reminisced about the grand old days of Poplar Grove, and she showed me the small vase sitting on a living room shelf that I had bought for her so many years before.

Caught up in the moment, I looked at her across the room and blurted out, "Grandma Leda, you haven't changed a bit."

Despite her age, her quick wit reared its head as she said, "You mean I always looked like a little old lady?"

We both laughed, but she knew what I meant. Her countenance, her love, and her faith remained unchanged-seeming to transcend time. And although I wasn't sitting in the presence of what the world would describe as royalty, I knew I was in the presence of nobility. Here was an elect daughter of God who had endured with grace the trials of life. While her humble living room was semi-dark, the room was full of her light and the light of Him whom she had so faithfully followed for so many years. I learned a great lesson from Grandma Leda: while she never possessed worldly renown or wealth, she was endowed with the knowledge and wisdom that come from a life of faith, service, and love. At the age of ninety she was still performing her duty—serving others, studying, praying, and being a neighbor and friend to all. When asked by the city how she felt about a men's halfway house being proposed around the corner, she simply said they would always be welcomed by her. True to her word, many a resident of that halfway house enjoyed Leda's cookies and conversations. One of the things that had a strong impact on me during that visit was how Grandma Leda, in the winter of her life, still remembered where she had come from. That particular trait helps to sustain our faith and keep us grounded.

Harry S. Truman, the thirty-third President of the United States, was a simple, plain-spoken man without much pretense from Independence, Missouri. Like my friend Leda Sampson, with Harry Truman, what you saw was what you got. He tried his hand at farming and then tried his hand in business when he bought a men's clothing store. Both efforts failed. Finally, at the age of thirty-eight, Truman found his niche when he was elected as a county judge. Twelve years later, in 1934, he was elected to the U.S. Senate and then in 1944 was elected as Franklin Delano Roosevelt's third vice president. Three months after their inauguration, Roosevelt died, and Truman was thrust onto the world stage as President of the United States. Within four short months he would make the difficult decision to drop two atomic bombs on Japan to usher in the conclusion of World War II.

Over the course of the next eight years, President Truman oversaw the rebuilding of Europe, authored what came to be known as the Truman Doctrine to contain communism, and staged one of the most stunning upsets in political history in 1948 when he came from behind to defeat the heavily favored Thomas Dewey, winning a second term. Great achievements from a simple man from Missouri. And yet through it all, Harry Truman remained the ultimate common man, stating, "I tried never to forget who I was and where I'd come from and where I would go back to."[8] Indeed, following his presidency, he returned with his wife to Independence, Missouri, to the same two-story white house they had lived in all their lives and the same morning walks around town he had always taken. His simple faith in himself and mankind helped Harry Truman be a father to an entire nation at a critical time when a common man was needed. That attitude, which would benefit today's politicians, has a great parallel to our view of this life.

Grandma Leda also knew who she was, where she came from, and where she was headed. In a mortal world full of confusion and questions, this lesson of faith and remembering the answers to those three questions is a blessing beyond comprehension. And it is a vital component in the development of happy, confident children.

I have often found it a challenge to act upon the principle of faith. At a basic level, I understand how it works. I understand that great faith can do anything; it can move mountains, raise the dead, and overcome any trial. Through the gospel of Jesus Christ, I know how everything will end, and I know that if I'm faithful in keeping my covenants, I can receive all that God has. However, acting upon that faith seems far more difficult. Fear of failure, fear of what others will think, and fear of the pain I may have to endure to await the glorious end—all these seem to envelop me in times of immediate crisis. It is in these times when our faith is tested that we really find out where God is and how He is preparing us for something far better than we can comprehend. In order for us to live with Him again, we must become like Him. We must develop the characteristics He possesses, and the foundation of these is faith.

A few years ago, we signed our younger children up for swimming lessons held in the backyard pool of our good friends. I decided to take advantage of a beautiful summer day to watch them and bask in the morning sun by the pool. As I watched my youngest son, Joseph, I suddenly realized that, rather than learning to swim, our water-apprehensive five-year-old was letting his overly kind swimming teacher carry him across the pool. In an attempt to help him float on his back, she walked along with her hands under his back while he lay there like a corpse. With trepidation in his voice, I heard him nervously ask her a question that I have asked so often during my times of trial. With all the confidence he could muster, Joseph said, "Am I there yet?" My anxious, fearful five-year-old, trying so hard to be brave and calm, was hoping he would arrive at his destination soon. In that innocent question, I realized that he was just like his anxious, fearful father. How often, when going through something exceedingly difficult, had I asked my Father in Heaven, "Am I there yet?" and hoped with the same earnestness that I was close to my destination.

These experiences always help me better understand the man who brought his son who suffered from a "dumb" spirit to the Savior. With his young son foaming at the mouth, he placed him on the ground at the feet of Jesus. When the Savior asked him how long he had suffered these afflictions, the father responded that his son had endured the fits since he had been a small child. He then proceeded to tell the Savior that the episodes would often send his son into the fire or into the waters where he could be destroyed. He then humbly said in Mark 9:22, "But if thou canst do any thing, have compassion on us, and help us." In Mark 9:23–24, "Jesus said unto him, If thou canst believe, all things are possible to him that believeth. And straightway the father of the child cried out, and said with tears, Lord, I believe; help thou mine unbelief." I can relate to that father. So often, during times of distress when I've stated my belief, I've still found myself needing the Lord to rescue me from my fears and doubts.

How comforting to know that the Lord understands and loves us so very much. Just as He healed this man's son, He will help us along with our sincere desires to turn unbelief into belief. What a message of peace.

Through all the trials we face, our faith continually grows, and we find that we're capable of so much more than we previously thought. Faith is the great tool of mortality. It creates worlds, it governs the laws of God, and His priesthood ordinances are contingent upon it.

I've always been amazed by the faith that came to the Apostle Peter. Here was a man who literally walked, talked, ate, and traveled with the Lord Jesus Christ. Peter observed the Lord in action and experienced the person-to-person conversations with the Savior that any devoted follower would give anything to have. And yet Peter, this companion of the Savior, seemed to have a greater conviction and greater faith after the Lord was gone than he did when he walked with Him. What happened to Peter? First, he received the gift and power of the Holy Ghost. Second, his faith had so developed that he paid the personal price to come to know God. Peter's faith no longer required him to see and be with the Lord to know that he was real. His conversion full, Peter was able to stand as a firm witness after the death and resurrection of Jesus Christ.

When it comes to tests of our faith, the Lord has always taught that we should not look for nor seek after signs of proof of his existence. The scriptures and the history of the Church of Jesus Christ are replete with examples of those who saw angels and yet did not remain faithful. Laman and Lemuel as well as witnesses of the plates of the Book of Mormon were given the privilege to see heavenly beings, and yet it seems their faith could not withstand the trials and tests of that faith. Seeing was not enough. Zeal was not enough. They needed to know the Lord deeply and they needed to have a belief in and a testimony of Him penetrating through their soul. As the world shifts and moves away from God at an alarming rate, it is vital that we have that same relationship with, faith in, and testimony of the Lord Jesus Christ.

Developing and exercising faith requires many things for us to act upon, and the first of these is a simple yet fundamental blessing our Heavenly Father provides us with: prayer. Moses 6:61 says, "Therefore it is given to abide in you; the record of heaven; the Comforter; the peaceable things of immortal glory; the truth of all things; that which quickeneth all things, which maketh alive all things; that which knoweth all things, and hath all power according to wisdom, mercy, truth, justice, and judgment." Just as the Lord created everything we would need in this life to support us physically, so He gave us everything we would need to support us spiritually. Prayer is the key that unlocks the heavens and enables us to receive all the promises above as well as all God has to bless us with.

In the October 2019 General Conference of The Church of Jesus Christ of Latter-day Saints, Elder Dale G. Renlund of the Quorum of the Twelve Apostles stated, "The only way faith grows is for an individual to act in faith. These actions are often prompted by invitations extended by others, but we cannot 'grow' someone else's faith or rely solely on others to bolster our own. For our faith to grow, we must choose faith-building actions, such as praying, studying the scriptures, partaking of the sacrament, keeping the commandments, and serving others."[9]

Second, fundamental to our faith is the recognition that we must rely on the Lord. Only when we obtain and accept that reliance can we fully accomplish all that He has for us to do and become who He knows we can become. Part of this teaching includes helping our children understand whom they should turn to. In a world that can easily sway our focus to material things and celebrities, the real source of joy and peace truly is the Savior.

In John 5:2–9 we read the following:

> Now there is at Jerusalem by the sheep market a pool, which is called in the Hebrew tongue Bethesda, having five porches.
>
> In these lay a great multitude of impotent folk, of blind, halt, withered, waiting for the moving of the water. For an angel went down at a certain season into the pool, and troubled the water: whosoever then first after the troubling of the water

stepped in was made whole of whatsoever disease he had. And a certain man was there, which had an infirmity thirty and eight years. When Jesus saw him lie, and knew that he had been now a long time in that case, he saith unto him, Wilt thou be made whole? The impotent man answered him, Sir, I have no man, when the water is troubled, to put me into the pool: but while I am coming, another steppeth down before me. Jesus saith unto him, Rise, take up thy bed, and walk. And immediately the man was made whole, and took up his bed, and walked.

This man lay by the pool each day, hoping for the opportunity to be the first in and be healed. However, without someone to help him, he had no way of getting to the pool before someone else could. When I remember this story, I picture Danish artist Carl Bloch's masterful painting *Christ Healing the Sick at Bethesda*. In it we see the Savior, lovingly pulling back a canopy that is partially covering this man while others wait close by for the troubling of the water. The Savior saw him in this crowd of infirm people and went to him. And while He knew the answer to His question, He still asked him, "Wilt thou be made whole?" This man of faith, diseased for thirty-eight years, could only utter the heartfelt plea, "Sir, I have no man." The Savior then "immediately" healed him. The Savior was his "man." And He is ours. In a world of trial, adversity, sadness, and heartache, we never need say, "Sir, I have no man." I thank God every day for that knowledge and the strength, peace, joy, and power that it brings.

Our journey through mortality has already been personalized for us by our loving and wise Heavenly Father. It requires growth which comes through trial. It is during these times that our faith is tested as the answers and ends we seek may not come as quickly as we would like them to. However, as we pray with our might and leave the rest to the Lord, our faith becomes strong, and we learn to rely on the Lord. We are molded as we become students in the Lord's tutoring program, which prepares us to receive all he has. And along the way, the Savior stands through it all, ready to lovingly pull back the canopy and say, "Wilt thou be made whole?"

Third, optimism is important in our development of faith. When we struggle, we are encouraged to count our blessings and find the good in our lives. President Henry B. Eyring of the First Presidency once stated that he ended each day by writing in his journal and recording how he had seen the hand of God in his life that day. That positive approach can make all the difference.[10]

Howard W. Hunter, the fourteenth president of The Church of Jesus Christ of Latter-day Saints, said this:

> As a being of power, intelligence, and the master of his own thoughts, a man holds the key to every situation, to make his life what he chooses it to be. When he discovers the divine power within his soul, he can lead his life to a God-like nature. If one dreams lofty dreams, so shall he become. There is magic in the way one thinks. If we expect the worst, we will get the worst. If we expect the best, we will receive the best. If we train our minds to have faith in God and ourselves, we are using one of the great laws of life. If we think and live righteously, happiness will find its place in our lives. It is amazing when we expect the best how forces are set in motion which cause the best to materialize. Our thoughts more than circumstances determine the course of our lives. Outward circumstances do not determine the course of our lives as much as the thoughts that habitually occupy our minds. These thoughts carve their impression on our faces, in our hearts, and on the tablet of our eternal souls.[11]

President Hunter's powerful words give us deeper insight into the principle of faith. The more we believe, the greater our peace. The greater our peace, the greater our hope; the greater our hope, the more positive we become. We believe in ourselves, and we believe in God. When we believe in God, we believe His promise that our faith can and will produce miracles. Then we follow what Elder Joseph B. Wirthlin taught when he said to do all we can and leave the rest to the Lord.[12]

From this place of faith, we grow closer to the Lord, and as we make covenants with Him and strive to keep them, they "create a sure foundation for spiritual progression," as Elder Renlund states.[13] This process is vital on our road to discipleship because those who choose to walk the path will, at some point in their journey, be asked to fully submit themselves to God. It is then that we experience what Moses and the brother of Jared experienced: our faith, obedience, and efforts are such that the Lord is unable to withhold His blessings. Moses, the brother of Jared, and others who saw God were not merely rewarded for their faith by seeing God. Their faith had developed so strongly that God could not hold back His blessings. And although we may not literally see God, we will most assuredly see Him by seeing His hands in our lives.

The light that comes from that level of faith brings peace to our lives. The fear and doubt that are hallmarks of the adversary's message simply cannot coexist with faith and peace. Satan knows that fear paralyzes us and destroys our faith. It then yields to doubt and despair, then to disbelief and disobedience. However, we possess the knowledge of God's plan for us. We know who we are and what our potential is. Furthermore, we know the plan's outcome. The Lord has already won. When remembered, this knowledge has the power to strengthen our faith and resolve while the perspective of what matters fills our hearts with peace.

The development of faith in our children is vital. They come so innocent and full of faith. They trust fully. And yet the more they experience the world and its hardness, the more important faith becomes.

I recall a moment in time with my son Stephen. As he sat close to me in our chapel awaiting his turn to be baptized, he said, "I'm scared,

Dad." I hugged him and told him that I would be right there the whole time and that there was nothing for him to be afraid of. Then as we sat quietly, I realized that the day would come when he would experience fear and loneliness and I would not be there. I was reminded then of the urgency to teach him where to turn for faith and peace and how to rely on prayer to obtain them. Eleven years later when he entered the Missionary Training Center, I reminded him of that episode and reminded him of the lessons of faith he had learned. In Doctrine and Covenants 84:88 the Lord said, "I will go before your face. I will be on your right hand and on your left, and my Spirit shall be in your hearts, and mine angels round about you, to bear you up." Stephen had learned who would always be there and whom he could always turn to.

JoAnn and I were reminded of this message at a park where we saw a young father with his four-year-old daughter. We watched as he put her on his shoulders, twirled her around, and pushed her on a swing. When he walked to their car just a few yards away to make a phone call, she began to follow him. Turning around, he encouraged her to keep playing. Despite his assurances that he could see her and that he would be right back, she continued to follow him. When she asked him if he was leaving her, he turned back to her, walked toward her, knelt, and lovingly said, "I promise that I will never leave you." With that, she smiled and began walking back to the play area. Still unsure, she would turn around every few feet to make sure he was still there. Finally, her faith in her father assured, she smiled and confidently went to the swing.

We witnessed a powerful lesson in that sweet moment. We discussed those times in our lives when, with anxiety and fear, we have appealed to our Heavenly Father with that same question: "Are you leaving me?" In those moments, the sweet reassurance has come from him who loves us beyond our comprehension with those words of peace: "I promise that I will never leave you." John 14:27 reads, "Peace I leave with you, my peace I give unto you: not as the world giveth, give I unto you. Let not your heart be troubled, neither let it be afraid." We were again reassured of the importance of expending all the energy possible to teach our children whom they could turn to and have faith in.

A few years ago, Grandma Leda's question of "Am I there yet?" was answered when, after ninety-seven years in mortality, her Heavenly Father called her home. When she passed through the veil, things of the world suddenly became insignificant. What mattered was the person she had molded into through her journey. It was the result of the premortal longing she'd had to become like God. It was her faith in that God, who had so carefully customized her journey, that enabled her to complete it. Now, her mortal journey finished, she lives on in the hearts of those who loved her and those whom she influenced with her great devotion of faith.

3

Perry Mason, Chocolate Stars, and the Perpetual Quilt

Lessons on Love

"Family lore told me Grandma Waterfield would have preferred a glass of Fisher beer."

One of the great murder mysteries of television's early "heydays" was a black-and-white drama called *Perry Mason*. This whodunit, mixing intrigue, revenge, and curveballs, ran gloriously from 1957 to 1966. An attorney by trade, Mason, played by Raymond Burr, was a model of efficiency, legal brilliance, and coolness under pressure. Aided by his loyal secretary, Della Street, and his trusty private eye sidekick Paul Drake, Mason always knew what to say at the right moment and always bested his rival, Hamilton Berger, the Los Angeles County district attorney. Regardless of the difficulty, each episode ended with the same exciting conclusion—Perry going for the jugular and drawing out a surprising confession from an unexpected murderer on the witness stand. It was classic television.

I loved *Perry Mason* as a young boy. When my parents went out, they would leave my sisters and me with one of our grandmothers. When it was my maternal grandmother's turn, we drove from Poplar Grove to my Grandma Markus's humble but cozy Midvale home with its small living room, smaller kitchen, two still smaller bedrooms, and an even smaller bathroom just inside the smaller still back porch. Her tiny living room gained fame as the home of *Perry Mason* reruns. Wide-eyed and somewhat anxious, I would sit right by her side as the ominous trumpet-pounding theme song opened the show against the backdrop of Grandma's house where every light was turned off. Among her many talents, Grandma Markus always knew how to set an effective stage where television murder was concerned. However, the fear factor of murder in black-and-white television was completely endurable when you were tucked closely at Grandma Markus's side. We knew this time was special, and with her arms around us, we knew we were loved.

I never had the influence of grandfathers in my life. My maternal grandfather passed away during my first year, and my paternal grandfather literally dropped dead in the living room of a ruptured aorta on my fifth New Year's Eve. Despite their loss, the lessons I learned from my grandmothers bridged that gap, and their examples changed my life.

My maternal grandmother, Jennie Louise Barben Markus, was a hard-working woman with a gift for giving to others. A farm girl raised in The Church of Jesus Christ of Latter-day Saints, she descended from Swiss immigrants who settled in Midway, Utah, a beautiful town on the other side of the mountains from the Salt Lake Valley. At the age of eighteen she married Max Markus, the son of a Croatian mother and a Serbian father, who immigrated to America and never learned to speak English. My grandfather was a jack-of-all-trades, and his work experience proved it. With property given him by his parents, my grandpa built a small home for them in Midvale's old avenue district just off Main Street, where they raised seven children in very humble circumstances.

Kind, quiet, and reserved, Grandma Markus had a softness that manifested itself when she made sure any hobo jumping off the trains that ran less than fifty yards from their home was given a meal on the front porch. Her cooking skills were incredible, and she could make a meal out of anything. Her compassion, and those delicious meals, led those hobos to "mark" her home as a place where future travelers would be welcome.

Although life was never easy, the Markus brand of humor became legendary. Her outward calmness belied a quick wit, a surprising sense of tenacity, and the ability to let someone "have it" if necessary. As with any other member of the Markus family, you knew where you stood with grandma. After she suffered a heart attack, I opened my fourteen-year-old big mouth and told her she needed to remember she wasn't a spring chicken anymore. She looked at me with that "hear it comes" smile and flatly told me she could still kick my rear end.

One of her greatest legacies was her work ethic. When my mom's younger sister Lucille started school, grandma took a job at a café where she worked from 9:00 to 4:00 and 6:00 to 9:00 six days a week. During her two-hour break, she walked home, fixed dinner for her family, and walked back to the café. Her one day off was spent cleaning the house, doing the laundry on their old wringer washing machine, and making Sunday dinner.

After my grandfather died, Grandma Markus kept working full time at Bern's Market on Midvale's downtown Main Street to support her and the two sons she still had at home. Her meager circumstances made her gifts of Christmas socks and the occasional silver dollar on my birthday all the more special. She was a woman of few words, and yet when she smiled and laughed, you could see love in her eyes. Her life was one of love, faith, endurance, service, and hard work. While she didn't have much materially to give, she gave all her heart.

On the flip side of the family was my grandma Amelia Waterfield Williams. While *Perry Mason* reigned at Grandma Markus's house, Grandma Williams was a *Gunsmoke* woman. Born in England, Amelia

Waterfield immigrated to the United States with her parents, brother, and sister when she was all of four years old. Raised in the coal camps of central Utah, she joined The Church of Jesus Christ of Latter-day Saints at age nineteen and met and married Neldon Williams. My grandpa, also a coal miner, had gone to work in the mines at the age of fourteen when his dad had died. After marrying my grandma, they lived in four different mining towns before finally settling in Castle Dale. When a broken leg made it necessary for him to leave the mines, he accepted work as a janitor at a school and did whatever odd jobs he could find while my grandmother earned money by doing laundry and ironing for people around town. They worked hard and had little. Seeking better work, they packed up and moved to Salt Lake in 1951.

After my grandfather passed away, Grandma Williams refused to quit. She went out and got her first driver's license and, wanting to stay busy, went to work full time, all at the age of sixty-seven. Of her two new activities, she mastered the latter with ease as a rug maker and worked full time for the next twenty-one years. As for her driving, after three failed attempts to pass the driving test, family opinion was soon unanimous that she was a vehicular catastrophe looking for a place to happen. When she couldn't figure out how to take her own driveway at less than thirty miles an hour, my dad, his three brothers, and his sister confiscated her license, sold the '63 Buick, and bought her a bus pass. Her driving career cut short, Grandma became a cog in the world of mass transit.

Always full of fun and optimism, Grandma Williams rode inner tubes behind my uncles' snowmobiles—laughing all the way—well into her seventies, and her love of life and her love for her family were hallmarks of her life. In the back bedroom of her west-side Salt Lake City home was evidence of that love. In her work as a rug maker, she would buy scraps of material and bring them home for what I called her perpetual quilt. Straddling the double bed were four quilting frames that always had a quilt in progress atop them. Once completed, she gave it away in sequence to a child or grandchild and threw on another one. She quilted to the end of her life, and to this day, those perpetual quilts give us all the gift of warmth that we always felt in her presence.

One of the benchmarks of love is service, and Grandma Williams's example taught me a great lesson. Her mother, my great-grandma Waterfield, moved to Salt Lake with her husband after he retired from the mines and bought a home one-half block from where my grandparents would later live. When Grandma Waterfield hit her nineties and became much less mobile, her three daughters—my grandma being one of them—took weekly turns taking care of her, getting her up, feeding her, and putting her to bed. For a period of time, I joined my grandmother on her afternoon visits and walked the half block to visit Grandma Waterfield.

Upon our arrival, she was always sitting on the living room sofa just where Grandma Williams had put her that morning. There from her perch she would send my grandma next door to Joe's, a small, corner neighborhood grocery store owned and operated by none other than Joe, for a bag of chocolate stars. I could never rattle off the entire inventory, but I knew Joe was a purveyor of milk, those delectable chocolate stars, Lucky Strike cigarettes, and Fisher beer. This insider knowledge was based on what Grandma Williams served me as well as what I knew Grandma Waterfield had smoked and drank earlier in her life. My grandma would return a few minutes later, go into the kitchen, and return with a cold glass of milk from the old refrigerator with the cooling unit on top and a plate of those chocolate stars. Grandma Waterfield herself had always been an aficionado of the aforementioned brand of beer; however, her advancing age had resulted in a doctor-led era of prohibition. So, there we sat, drinking milk while I ate those delicious chocolate stars. Despite her smile, family lore told me Grandma Waterfield would have preferred a glass of Fisher beer.

My grandma Waterfield didn't speak much, and her feeble condition made her tire quickly, but I remember how much love I felt from her. She would ask me how I was and listen to whatever conversation I made. Chocolate stars and cold milk never tasted better. It was a contribution from my frail, couch-bound great-grandmother who wanted to offer me something special. And I learned from my seventy-plus-year-old grandmother that serving and taking care of her mother was a joyful part of her life. Some years later as Grandma Williams approached the end of her life, I spent some of the best evenings of my life visiting her each week when I had college classes in Salt Lake. When I drove into her driveway, there she stood, waiting for me at the screen door with a just-cooked TV dinner sitting on an old metal fold-out TV table by the couch. In all these experiences, I learned that *Grandma* means love, and Great-Grandma Waterfield, Grandma Williams, and Grandma Markus each influenced my life and provided great lessons to follow in my role as a father.

Love is arguably the most important human emotion. Further, it is the characteristic that drives everything that our Heavenly Father and the Savior do for us. In 1 Corinthians 13:13 the Apostle Paul taught about the importance of charity, the pure love of Christ, when he said, "And now abideth faith, hope, charity, these three; but the greatest of these is charity."

And yet love seems so often to be lacking in today's world. Consider the characteristics spawned from love: tolerance, patience, understanding, grace, mercy, and selflessness. When those additional traits are studied, it's easy to see how far the world drifts from the love we should have for each other. Our society today is so focused on power, self-satisfaction, ambition, and achievement that love is often forgotten and viewed as a weakness. In political and business circles, people work hard to smear the character and credibility of others who oppose them without any thought or concern for that person. This lack of civility and respect and the speed at which these slanders run throughout the media have resulted in a jaded, distrustful society.

George Washington's life was guided by 110 rules of civility that he learned as a sixteen-year-old, and those rules served as the foundation of his entire life. Often referred to as the father of our country, Washington led the Continental Army during the American Revolution that lasted five long years. Countless stories tell of his sacrifices for his men and of his ability to lead and inspire so many when the future looked so bleak. Later, when the Constitution was written and adopted, he agreed to serve as the nation's first president to help ensure the document's passage.

Throughout Washington's life, he understood the importance of setting a proper beginning. His understanding of his place in history as well as his responsibility as the nation's first president came from a wisdom that swelled from deep within. As the leader of a new nation that was to be unlike any other in history, he knew he was setting a precedent with everything he did. His refusal to serve more than two terms was so impactful that no president attempted a third term until Franklin D. Roosevelt in 1940, 144 years later. (It wasn't until 1947 that the twenty-second amendment would limit a president by law to two terms.) When I think of Washington's ability and foresight to place the needs of those for whom he had responsibility above his own desires or hopes, I am in awe of his greatness. That lesson is one of greatness, for surely his life was an extreme expression of love, civility, and kindness.

I do believe that most people in the world are good, decent, and caring despite what we see in politics, world conflict, and greed. However, as in every case, the world is only one generation from either upward or downward societal trends. One of the most important things we can teach our children is love. Love for each other, love for themselves, love for their neighbor, and love for God.

The logical place where love should begin is the love that husbands have for their wives. In an October 2011 General Conference talk, Elaine Dalton, a former Young Women General President of The Church of Jesus Christ of Latter-day Saints, said, "How can a father raise a happy, well-adjusted daughter in today's increasingly toxic world?" She answered with an oft-repeated statement made by former Church President David O. McKay, who said, "The most important thing a father can do for his [daughter] is to love [her] mother."[14] Among the many lessons I learned from my dad, perhaps the most important was that he showed me how to value women. In him, I saw a man who loved my mother, respected my mother, built up my mother, and supported my mother. Together, they worked side by side to bless and take care of the five children sent to their home.

The importance of loving our wives is vital in that it shows our sons and daughters the high expectations God places upon the treatment of His daughters. Our Heavenly Father created man and woman and foreordained them to lead in righteousness together. The Lord's teachings always have been and always will be that His sons and daughters are equal. In putting into place His plan for us, God gave both His sons and daughters responsibilities to bless their children during their sojourn in mortality. Each is blessed with character traits and abilities that complement each other, enabling them to lead their families together. With that comes the opportunity to teach Christlike attributes as well as patterns of goodness, love, respect, and generosity, in the home. And when we understand the importance of obtaining a body in God's plan for each of His children, we gain insight into the sacred role of motherhood.

Our world today portrays women in such polarizing ways that confusion seems to run rampant regarding their role. So many in our society twist women's sexuality and sell pornography in ways that ruin men's image of women and portray them as mere objects. These images demean the daughters of God, give young girls unrealistic views of their own self-worth, and taint men's views of noble womanhood. We must learn to temper our physical appetites and express appreciation for the many forms of beauty that exist in all women—inside and out. If we cannot, then we're contributing to the societal pressures of physical beauty that our daughters face, and we're not setting the standard we hope our sons will achieve.

Others are so intent on leveling the entire playing field between men and women that they reduce to insignificance some of the great, noble, and innate traits that make a woman so strong. My life is enhanced by JoAnn's ability to endure and lift as well as her compassion and determination. Her qualities temper me and help me meet life's challenges, and I strive each day to do the same for her. Without her I am incomplete. And without her character and her attributes, I am incapable of becoming all who God intends me to become.

Further evidence of the adversary's attacks on women comes in the form of the world's marginalizing the role of a mother. Once considered to be of utmost importance, the world today tells women that motherhood is often menial and not enough. In fact, many suggest that women who focus on motherhood are robbing themselves of success and hampering the equality movement for all women. Those who choose to apply their greatest efforts toward family and children are too often looked down upon. How easy it seems to put aside the thought that the continuation of our society, and any blessings we receive from it, are contingent upon the raising of capable, bright, and contributing successive generations.

I'm not advocating a retreat from the societal changes that have improved life for women. They have so much to offer, and women around the world have made and are making great contributions in business, medicine, science, education, and leadership, just to name a few. The world needs their abilities and, as fathers, we must help our wives and our daughters, along with our sons, become all they can become. One of the greatest things we can do for our children is to help them and encourage them to accomplish their dreams and learn that, with God, anything is possible. We must, however, defend and esteem the nobility of women and ensure we aren't doing anything in our conduct that would demean, devalue, or demoralize the elect daughters of God or the role of motherhood.

One year, just prior to a wedding anniversary, I realized the impact of this love when I stopped at a store to pick up some flowers for my wife. My daughters Julee, Emma, and Eliza, ages twelve, eleven, and eight at the time, decided to wait in the car with their older brothers. When I walked out to the car, carrying the flowers, I unlocked and opened the door to the sound of clapping and cheering. My three daughters were so happy that I had bought flowers for their mother that they were unable to contain their emotions. I looked at their big, beautiful smiles and clapping hands and was humbled by the joy they received by seeing me love their mother.

Love for your spouse accomplishes many things. First, it strengthens marital relationships, which in turn strengthens families. The more love we show, the more our love grows and the easier it is for us to overcome differences and look past flaws. Love also strengthens our resolve to be faithful so we won't be among those whom the ancient prophet Jacob proclaimed had sought riches and were unfaithful to their wives. In a powerful sermon on the negative impacts of a father's bad choices, he said in Jacob 2:35, "Behold, ye have done greater iniquities than the Lamanites, our brethren. Ye have broken the hearts of your tender wives, and lost the confidence of your children, because of your bad examples before them; and the sobbings of their hearts ascend up to God against you. And because of the strictness of the word of God, which cometh down against you, many hearts died, pierced with deep wounds."

When I seriously contemplate how my bad choices could break JoAnn's heart and cause me to lose the confidence of my children—in other words, destroy my family and compromise and ruin everything I love—I find myself shaking at the very thought of sin. In 2 Nephi 4:26–35, Nephi provided his great anthem to glorying and trusting in God. When we trust in God, rejoice in Him, and cry unto Him with a broken heart and a contrite spirit, we will be, as Nephi stated, delivered from our enemies and encircled by the Lord's robes of righteousness. We must do all we can to fortify our families, for those responsibilities are the greatest we as husbands and fathers have been given. Then, as we spend time with our wives, attend the temple together, pray together, and seek each other's counsel in all things, that love will strengthen and grow until we will understand the true meaning of the phrase *help meet* as told in the book of Genesis.

That love in a home then creates an environment of stability and peace, a haven from the world where our children can be accepted and loved and grow in confidence. When our children see us happy and loving, it makes it easier for them to confidently evaluate relationships, improve, and grow into adulthood. In that atmosphere, children may learn to love themselves for who they are.

Witnessing the birth of each of our children has been a great spiritual experience as I have seen them take their first breath and have felt an immediate rush of love, knowing that I would give or do anything for them. And while the emotions and expressions of love come at different times and in different ways to all of us, I assure you that the love for your children will come. As we express love in our own way and follow our instincts and impressions, the love our children need will begin to flow from us. Then, in our role as parents, we will be given a glorious glimpse of how much God loves each of us. For, as certain as we want to give our children all we have, so does He want to give all of us all He has.

When Lehi had his dream of the "Tree of Life," his thoughts immediately turned to his family. These were the God-given feelings of a patriarch who understood his greatest calling. He partook of the fruit—the love of God—and it filled his soul "with exceedingly great joy" (1 Nephi 8:12), such joy that he couldn't wait to have his family taste it. He knew what it was and knew what it would do for them. Lehi knew the love of God was truly the only thing that would bring lasting happiness.

The love of God is a vital component of the formula that enables God's children to live in the world and yet not be of it. When Nephi interpreted Lehi's dream, he clarified, among other things, that the river of water his father had seen represented the filthiness of the world. In 1 Nephi 15:27, Nephi talked about Lehi and told his brothers that "so much was his mind swallowed up in other things that he beheld not the filthiness of the water." The fruit Lehi had partaken of had so changed his life and filled his heart with love that he didn't even notice the filthiness of the river that flowed by him. That same love of God can be a great blessing to our children as they strive to remain strong in a world filled with filthy waters.

Knowing who we are and that God loves us is necessary in our efforts to wrestle with acceptance in a world where physical beauty seems to be everything. One morning JoAnn and I paused in the hallway of our home to watch our then four-year-old daughter dancing in her princess dress while singing songs from Disney's *Sleeping Beauty*. As we stood taking in the moment, Emma, upon seeing us, said, "I'm a princess." We looked at her beautiful smiling face and said, "Yes Emma, you are a princess." Reminding our children that they are princesses and princes is a necessity, for surely the day will come when someone tries to convince them they're not.

The greatest example of love we have is the love of our Heavenly Father and our Savior. Their love is almost unimaginable when we truly consider what the Savior did for each of us as well as the fact that His Father allowed Him to do it. Their love is so universal, and yet it is also so personal. J. Devn Cornish, a member of the Second Quorum of the Seventy for The Church of Jesus Christ of Latter-days Saints, once recounted an event from his life when he was a struggling resident surgeon at the Boston Children's Hospital. After an exceptionally long shift one day, he jumped on his mode of transportation, a bicycle, and began his ride home to his wife and children eagerly awaiting an energetic father. Tired, hungry, and out of money, he related the experience of a prayer he uttered and had answered when he found a quarter on the sidewalk that enabled him to buy a simple piece of chicken.

Of the experience, he stated:

> In His mercy, the God of heaven, the Creator and Ruler of all things everywhere, had heard a prayer about a very minor thing. One might well ask why He would concern Himself with something so small. I am led to believe that our Heavenly Father loves us so much that the things that are important to us become important to Him, just because He loves us. How much more would He want to help us with the big things that we ask, which are right (see 3 Nephi 18:20)?[15]

That story paints for me a very personal and intimate view of our relationship to our Father in Heaven. He is not some distant being observing our behavior from a view of superiority. He knows us on a deep level. His proximity is close, and He stands waiting to help and lift us with a love for and an interest in us that is beyond anything we can comprehend. As I consider the answers that have come to my simple prayers, I've come to see that what is important to me does indeed become important to Him.

It is in our Father and in His Son where we see the greatest testaments of love. John 3:16 reads, "For God so loved the world, that he gave his only begotten Son, that whosoever believeth in him should not perish, but have everlasting life." The Savior came into the world to teach, minister, and perform miracles before fulfilling His ultimate mission. After His indescribable experience in the Garden of Gethsemane, He was betrayed by Judas, accused of falsehoods, and taken to Pilate, then across Jerusalem to Herod, and then back to Pilate before being delivered to the masses who crucified Him. Three days later, He completed His work on our behalf when He rose from the dead and walked.

Teaching our children of their Heavenly Father's and Savior's love for them will fill their lives with light and hope, as the days will come when they will feel lonely, unloved, and forgotten. The knowledge that there is a God in the heavens who loves them beyond comprehension, that they are His children, and that He knows them intimately is necessary for them to endure the tests that are sure to come. Our Heavenly Father's feelings of fatherly, personal love toward us are evident in a statement made by the Quorum of the Twelve Apostles, who wrote, "Of all the titles of respect and honor and admiration that are given to deity, he has asked us to address Him as Father."[16]

The love of my grandmothers is a pivotal part of the foundation upon which my life has been built. These three small women, in the winter of their lives, loved and influenced me in the springtime of mine, and in them I saw and felt the love of my Heavenly Father. I know He placed me with them for a purpose because their love for me was unconditional and their joy in my joy was profound. And through it all, their love gave me a glimpse into the eternities and showed me how to share my love with the children who would one day be mine.

4
Florence and Howard Eva and Dick
Lessons on Knowledge

"The chance that in marriage she will draw a blockhead I calculate at about fourteen to one."

When Brigham Young's vanguard company first entered the Salt Lake Valley in July of 1847, he led them to the site of today's City and County Building in downtown Salt Lake City to camp for the night. Their first impressions of their arid new home must have stood in stark contrast to the lush, verdant landscapes of the places they had left behind. However, this vast valley, surrounded by mountains and the Great Salt Lake, was to be their home. Here they would build a city and plant crops and trees that would be fed by irrigated waters stemming from the many mountain creeks nearby.

Within a few days of their arrival, Brigham Young and other members of the Quorum of the Twelve staked out the site for the temple before getting down to the business of building homes and planting crops for the coming winter. With the temple block serving as the center point for their city of Zion, Salt Lake City began to rise. Based on a grid system, the city's streets, and ultimately those of its future suburbs, formed a plan of perfectly square blocks with numbered streets moving from the temple block in all directions—north, south, east, and west. Future generations would come to see the ease of calculating how many blocks they lived from the city's core block by simply looking at their numerical street addresses.

As the city grew with both residents and commercial enterprises, farming ventures gravitated to the city's edges, establishing Salt Lake City's first non-downtown neighborhoods. One of these was an area just to the southwest near the Jordan River which, after an industrious pioneer's family planted a grove of poplar trees in the late 1800s, became known as Poplar Grove.[17] The turn of the century found more residents moving from the commercially oriented downtown blocks, and by the time the 1930s rolled around, Poplar Grove was experiencing a small housing boom that would run through the 1950s. By the time my parents married and were ready to purchase their first home during my second year, this thriving, established neighborhood was ready to greet them with open arms. Finding the home of their young dreams on safe, sleepy 700 South, they swooped in with a down payment and moved us into a remarkable world where four individuals would make a lasting impact on my life.

As the newest members of the Poplar Grove First Ward, my parents found a group of people leaning heavily toward middle age and above who were just waiting to make us a part of their family. With our new neighborhood came a plethora of opportunities for me to be completely spoiled. Our neighbors to the west were Florence and Howard Eugster. Before I knew her, Florence had been an accomplished tennis player and a member of the Mormon Tabernacle Choir (as it was called at the time). To us, she was our grandmotherly neighbor who, despite only being in her fifties, happily accepted us and took great care of us. She was both a highly trained nurse and an accomplished cook, and we learned quickly that her bright yellow kitchen was the place for any cure we needed. With any dessert functioning as a distraction, she would bandage me up and send me on my way.

Her husband Howard was a stand-up comic in waiting and a friend to everyone. The best storyteller of my young life, he always had a new adventure to share about growing up on Salt Lake City's west side. Whether he was in his garage fixing anything and everything or taking me to see the large locomotive engine in Pioneer Park, Howard had epic stories at the ready of his own childhood spent traversing the city's railroad tracks. Filling out the family was their always-smiling daughter JoAnn, who drove a great-looking dark green Corvair, and their cool-as-a-leather-jacket son John, who raced me around Poplar Grove on the back of his black and chrome motorcycle.

Behind our house, via a quick trip through the alley, was Florence's older sister, Eva Hansen, and their younger brother, Dick. Bachelorette and bachelor, kind, soft-spoken Eva and steady Dick lived together in a quaint light-brown bungalow on Wasatch Avenue that became my first breakfast haunt. I was always free to use the back door, and I would rush in and bound up the few steps leading to Eva's white and light-blue kitchen, where I would sit at her table by the east-facing window with the morning sunlight pouring in on my face. Fluffy scrambled eggs and toast never tasted better, especially when Eva's raspberry preserves were plastered all over her homemade bread. However, those who knew Eva never underestimated her. The oldest of her siblings, Eva was strong and determined with a diverse life's experience that included work in the motion picture studio business.

Dick was likewise determined. When he took a job running a jackhammer just after graduating from high school, one day was all it took for Dick to realize he wanted something different. So off he went to the University of Utah where he graduated from their engineering school. Although he travelled the world for the mining company he worked for,

Dick was quiet and humble. When he was home, he could be found in one of three places: reading in his refreshingly cool basement bedroom, working in the yard, or driving me around town in a sturdy light-green International.

After our family moved to Riverton, Dick and Eva's back bedroom became my very own quarters when my parents allowed me to spend a few days with Florence and Howard and Eva and Dick. They loved me, and oh how I loved them. Of all my memories of Poplar Grove, the time I spent with this influential foursome stands out as some of the sweetest. They accepted me for who I was, believed in me, and made me feel like the most important person in the world. When I told them I wanted to be President of the United States, they told me, and everyone else, that I had it in me to do it. They also pushed me to do my best in my interests and introduced me to new things. My love of hockey began in Eva and Dick's living room, where I would sit with them and listen to Jim Fisher call the old Salt Lake Golden Eagles hockey games on the small table radio.

Perhaps the most important thing they ever did for me was encourage my love of learning. My own thirst for knowledge began at a young age. I was a voracious reader, and I became an ardent student of American history at the age of eight when my dad brought home a book on the presidents of the United States. I read it cover to cover and was hooked. Among the cadre of people who helped fuel my passion for history and knowledge were my four grandparent-like friends from Poplar Grove. When they saw my interest in history, they poured gas on it. On my visits they would take me to every historical site in Salt Lake and encourage me to learn what had occurred there. My first forays to Salt Lake City's Beehive House, Utah's State Capitol Building, and the old ZCMI store's Tiffin Room for lunch were all planned and executed by Florence and Howard and Eva and Dick.

During one of these outings, I found out how much they believed in me. When we walked into the old Deseret Book store on Salt Lake's downtown South Temple Street, I spotted a book on the United States' presidents that I wanted more than anything. When Eva and Florence went to buy it for me and the clerk suggested it was beyond my reading level, Eva succinctly expressed that I was most likely a better reader than the clerk was. When we sauntered back onto South Temple, I left the store toting a morale victory and the book I wanted. Their love for me, as well as their enthusiasm for my interests, left a noticeably big imprint on my young life.

Aristotle stated that "the difference between a learned man and an ignorant one is the same as that between a living man and a corpse." In Doctrine and Covenants 93:36 the Lord states, "The glory of God is intelligence, or, in other words, light and truth." That glory has blessed mankind through the ages both spiritually and temporally with doctrines of truth that have lifted the poor, taught the ignorant, soothed the soul, propelled advancement, and enhanced life's quality.

Men and women have worked and sought since the time of Adam and Eve to achieve the riches and accolades of the world despite the obvious fact that we can take none of it with us when our time comes to leave this earth. Knowledge, relationships, life's experiences—those are the things we take with us when we depart this world. Once knowledge is gained, it is ours forever.

In October of 1988, President Thomas S. Monson gave a talk entitled "Hallmarks of a Happy Home," where he discussed the importance of learning and quoted celebrated author James A. Michener, who says, "A nation becomes what its young people read in their youth. Its ideals are fashioned then, its goals strongly determined." In encouraging us to have good books in our homes, President Monson also read from Doctrine and Covenants 88:118, "Seek ye out of the best books words of wisdom; seek learning, even by study and also by faith."[18]

The very foundation of our nation and its success hinges on the education and abilities of its generations. The more I read about America's great people and the contributions they've made, the more I desire to leave things better than I found them. And to do that requires knowledge. Before I ever became a father, I determined that one of the most important things I could do for my children, both sons and daughters, was to encourage their pursuit of knowledge. And while multiple paths prepare us for desired vocations, the journey of continual learning can help our children be well-rounded and secure in their knowledge of many things. Whether they learn through technical training, advanced degrees, or courses of self-taught individual learning, their education should be a life-long pursuit that leads them to excel in doing things well.

You don't need to be a college professor to teach your children. Your life experiences as well as your chosen paths of learning have created a wealth of knowledge you can share with them. Help them identify their strengths and encourage them in their areas of interest. The world needs all our diverse talents, and your children were sent to you by a Father in Heaven who has confidence in you. A quick look through history or even a glance around your community will identify paths to achievement with varying forms of education. The common denominator is that each successful person pursued a continual path of learning.

One of the best examples I have of the differing approaches to achieving learning is in my own father and father-in-law. My dad was part of his family's first generation that would attend a university. He accepted any work he could find, including janitorial and waste management. Yes, he was a garbage man so he could obtain a college degree. His efforts were rewarded when he graduated in education and found a career in accounting and later, risk management. As one career change led to another, his ability to learn and grasp different concepts in business enabled his success and development. Meanwhile, my father-in-law's path was a world apart. With a formal education that concluded with high school, his mechanical abilities became legendary. His belief that anything was possible enhanced his abilities and enabled his success in areas ranging from inventing a new industrial pump to building his own home. He defined the phrase "Where there's a will, there's a way." Despite their different journeys, each man had a quest for continual learning.

I knew I had a partner in learning when, on a trip to Boston, JoAnn bought a slew of books for the children we didn't have yet. When we built our first home, we combined our books and continued to build a family library with a place where our children would be able to read. In our case, our brightly sun-lit living room became our library and, as our children came, our collection became one of a variety of topics based on the interests of each child. Today our shelves are full of books that range from mechanics to innovation, from history to classics, from mysteries to adventure, and from biographies to doctrine.

As each of your children will develop interests in different areas, identify a place in your home, formal or casual, a room unto itself or a quiet corner, and fill it with books that your children will read. Also, spend time reading with them and see the memories it will create. My three college-age sons still talk about the time, many years ago, when with Matthew and Johnathan at my side and Stephen on my back, I lay on the floor of their bedroom and read Treasure Island to them. Added to this are the numerous images and memories of their mother constantly reading to them. Remember that, as a parent, you're always teaching. Of all the things you can leave your children, some of the most important things you'll leave will be those things you taught them.

The blessings of knowledge are vast. Knowledge enables our children to better understand differences of opinion and philosophy, which, in turn, enables them to express their views more profoundly with understanding and compassion. Education enables them to converse intelligently on many topics, which, in turn, enables them to be wise spokespersons and speak with confidence when the situations and opportunities arise. Further, it enables them to process world events and understand their impact upon their lives.

Today we have vast amounts of information at our fingertips, and unfortunately, social media, the internet, and news sources don't always have the right answers. So much of our news, tweets, and posts are biased, sensationalized, untrue, and downright hateful. How do we know what to believe? In a world where a Flintstones rerun often seems more factual than the news, we must learn to study and research and know where to go to get the real facts. With knowledge in tow, our children will learn to contribute to society and be good, responsible citizens.

Education also enables our children to understand so much more of God's workings, for surely the concepts of science, mathematics, history, and other topics go beyond this world. In addition, history enables us to better understand the past so we can avoid making the same mistakes. Winston Churchill, Great Britain's dynamic prime minister during World War II, said this of history: "The longer you can look back, the farther you can look forward."[19]

Of significant importance to me has been the educating of my daughters. Women have so much to offer, and their unique perspectives provide great enlightenment. Today's world needs the influence of women more than ever. Additionally, education provides them with the security, confidence, and assurance that they can make it on their own. In 1783 Thomas Jefferson, one of America's great founding fathers, was elected as a delegate from Virginia to the Congress of the Confederation, America's pre-constitution congress. When Jefferson left his Monticello estate to take office in Philadelphia, he was accompanied by his oldest child, eleven-year-old Patsy. Once in Philadelphia, he arranged for her to live in the educated home of Mrs. Thomas Hopkinson, where he left detailed instructions for her rigorous course of study. In *Thomas Jefferson: A Life* published in 1993, author Willard Sterne Randall detailed a letter Jefferson wrote to Francois Barbe-Marbois, secretary to the French legation in Philadelphia, explaining his detailed attention to Patsy's education. Intent on preparing her to lead a family on her own, Sterne wrote that Jefferson "did not want her to have to depend on a husband to solve all her problems and educate her own children."[20]

The shining new America of the 1780s was a rural, agrarian society surrounding the country's three population centers of Boston, New York, and Philadelphia. Collegiate-level education was reserved mostly for the privileged, and most went through life largely uneducated by today's standards. In a time when leadership, opportunity, and decision making were completely left to men, the idea of girls obtaining an education was largely considered to be a waste of time. Jefferson's differing viewpoint to such thinking emerged in the letter to Barbe-Marbois when he wrote concerning Patsy, "The chance that in marriage she will draw a blockhead I calculate at about fourteen to one."[21] Jefferson had done the math, so to speak, and who was going to question him? My question to Jefferson and my daughters today would be, if the odds were fourteen to one in 1783, what are they now?

The need for fathers to educate their sons and daughters has possibly never been more prevalent. America's role as a world leader depends upon their excellence. The world's societal needs depend upon their contributions. Our path to happiness depends upon their ability to preserve our freedom. The moral treatment of spouses, children, family, friends, and the world depends upon their civility and their nobility. The need to lift and build others depends upon their character. The growth of God's work depends upon their inspiration. The importance of knowledge doesn't end at the pursuit of a career and providing for one's family. That's only the tip of the iceberg. The gift of knowledge is contribution—leaving everything we touch in a better state than we found it.

Florence and Howard and Eva and Dick have long since passed on; however, their lessons of learning impact me to this day. On the day we left Deseret Book with my new book on the presidents in hand, Eva and Florence stopped me on the sidewalk, looked down at me, and said, "Always remember, you can accomplish whatever you want to do. And remember, never stop learning." Their influence upon my young mind enhanced my thirst for knowledge and stirred my desire for a journey that continues to this day.

— 5 —

Four Widows and a Blue Ford Falcon

Lessons on Service

"Duane, I'm going to come to your house and shoot out the porch light!"

My paternal grandfather began working in the coal mines of central Utah at the young age of fourteen when his father passed away. With only a widow's pension of $7.50 a month to support my great-grandmother and her seven children, it became my grandfather's responsibility as the oldest son to drop out of school and help provide for the family. Within a few years, he would marry and continue his work as a coal miner.

Coal mining was a nomadic life. Each mining company established and built an entire town or camp at or near the base of the new site. These miners and their families lived in these company-owned coal camps, rented company-owned houses, and shopped at the company-owned store where their purchases, often at inflated prices, were deducted from their pay. Once tapped out, they closed the mine, tore down the camp, and moved on to the next location. It was in this setting, in the long-gone coal-mining town of Heiner, Utah, where my dad was born. A few years later they moved about forty miles down the highway to Castle Dale, a small town of eight hundred in the central Utah county of Emery, where my dad grew up.

He loved Castle Dale. Throughout his life, he told stories of riding horses in the summer, sledding down snow-laden streets and hills in the winter, and sitting in the back of the car with his younger brother watching my grandparents dance at the town's tennis courts every Saturday night.

When he was twelve years old, he went to work on a neighboring farm and rewarded himself each payday by making weekly pilgrimages to Hunter's Drug Store, where he sat at the soda fountain counter and threw back chocolate malts. This love for Castle Dale created a desire in him to live in a place where his children might enjoy a similar environment. So, when the opportunity presented itself just before my eighth birthday, my parents made the difficult decision to leave our beloved Poplar Grove and move to the southwest area of the Salt Lake Valley to the then small town of Riverton.

This small hamlet would see me grow to adulthood and be influenced by the power of service. Farmland separated us from any neighboring towns. Everyone knew everyone, and the tradition of serving others was ingrained among the many generational agricultural families.

One of the greatest lessons we can teach our children is the importance of serving others. And there is no better example of service than what we learn from the earthly ministry of the Savior. While he was born into mortality to complete the ultimate acts of the Atonement, he also came to show us the way. If there were to be any questions as to how each of us should conduct ourselves, his examples in life would provide us with numerous precedents. When it came to service, the best way to describe his works is found in Acts 10:38, which simply states of the Lord that he "went about doing good."

Indeed, service is not only an example of a Christlike attribute—it is an essential prerequisite in our eternal character development. We have no need to question how our Heavenly Father feels about service. The Savior said, "The Son can do nothing of himself, but what he seeth the Father do" (John 5:19). Among His many Godlike characteristics, Jesus saw His Father serve, and so He did the same. Through those words we better understand Their relationship and learn another trait of fatherhood. Everything we do must be worthy of emulation by our sons and daughters. Therefore, if we want our children to learn to serve, we must serve.

When we moved in, Riverton's population of just less than three thousand people made it the near-perfect small-town environment Dad wanted. Loaded with charm, as small towns can be, it did cause a stir when we discovered that Riverton's only market, Peterson's Food Town, closed at 6:00 p.m. This created a crisis of sorts since my mom typically closed out each day with a shot of Pepsi, and we were the beneficiaries of candy when dad made mom's late-night contraband runs. However, as our good fortune would have it, the Wheel Inn Café around the corner on Redwood Road was open late, and what a place it was. You could order burgers and malts from the outside walk-up window, the counter inside, or the tables in the back by the jukebox. The restaurant was a classic, and it began my lifelong quest of finding the best off-the-beaten-path burger joints. Another unassuming candy destination was Beckstead Oil on the northeast corner of Redwood Road and 12600 South, where Leonard Beckstead would walk out, fill up the gas tank, and slip a roll of lifesavers to whoever had won the bruising battle of who got to sit in the back seat on the driver's side. We quickly learned that this was a man of true greatness.

The highlight of the year was Riverton's "Town Days" celebration held every Fourth of July. A cornucopia of small-town tradition, the day's activities were announced by a guy named Roy Litson, who drove around town in his old model, wood-paneled, dark-green Chevrolet truck with a megaphone temporarily attached to its roof. Known to call people out of bed as he drove by their house, this guy made P. T. Barnum look like an amateur. The food for Town Days was the ultimate in picnic cuisine—hamburgers and hot dogs grilled by the Riverton stake high council in Riverton Park's mess hall, a building with a cinderblock base topped with white painted wooden slats and shutters. What the high council most likely lacked in food handling credentials was more than made up for in atmosphere. These guys grilled and threw around slapstick as well as anyone.

The festivities kicked off on the eve of the Fourth with the traditional small-town parade complete with candy-throwing dignitaries, little league baseball teams, marching bands, and a slew of kids riding bicycles loaded with streamers. The next day began with a sunrise breakfast and flag ceremony and concluded with a firework show that was guaranteed to have a few warning shots sprayed into the crowd. Through each event, Roy Litson sat dutifully in his wood-paneled truck providing comedy and play-by-play commentary. Sandwiched in between all this were carnival rides, a little league baseball game, and a horseshoe throwing contest. Riverton's Fourth of July celebration was a sea of old-time Americana.

Each of us is shaped by different experiences and different events. Don't despair over difficult upbringings. Remember that the Savior's Atonement is designed to level the playing field of our experiences and negate those negative experiences. Just as important, you have the opportunity to create a great childhood for your children that you'll enjoy as much as they will.

My parents built a home in a new subdivision among the farms and older homes in Riverton's Second Ward, where we attended church in a wonderful old chapel on Redwood Road just north of the now-gone Beckstead Oil. Completed in 1929 at a cost of $55,000 of hard-earned cash from ward members, the church's dark-brown brick exterior ceremoniously looked over the green lawn, mature trees, and towering flagpole flying Old Glory's bursting colors in front. Inside, the building's stately yet cozy chapel was accented by dark-brown wood, tall north and south facing windows, a forty-foot-high vaulted ceiling, and a classic pulpit with three rows of tiered plush seats set in front of a tall arched window.[22] When the setting sunlight blazed through that west-facing, arched window, the painting of the Savior that hung near the arched portion was bathed in light creating a remarkable dramatic effect. As if the pulpit needed more ambiance, the organ occupied a snug corner roost that, despite seeming to be perfect, looked much like an afterthought. Every time I walked by that old organ, I wondered if it was left out of the original blueprints, a notion that added to the building's character.

From a demographic standpoint, the old Second Ward was loaded with storied families who gave the ward its distinguished character. We were led by Bishop Joseph Butterfield, who pulled you in with his sincere smile, firm handshake, and stories from his youth. He was an amazing father, both to his family and to our ward. A life-long entrepreneur, he dropped out of school as a teenager to support his family when his father died. Through his life, he farmed, owned a coal transport business, two car dealerships, a grocery store, an ice cream shop, and a laundromat. When times were difficult, he would sell parcels of land to provide for his large family, even though it meant sacrificing long-term gains. He understood the role of a patriarch and knew his priority was serving his family, not long-term financial gains.

Under Bishop Joe's watchful eye, week after week, Sundays became a pageantry of memorable stories from the likes of Vernon and Annette Jensen as well as the distinct, lyrical alto voices of Bishop Butterfield's daughters, Darla and Trenna, singing perfect harmony two rows behind us in the chorus for "Let Us All Press On." Meanwhile, with Que Butterfield manning the baton, the music played on. The son of another Butterfield, Rosamond—who gave voice and piano lessons to over five hundred children whether they could pay for it or not, Que could never resist the urge to lead us in his favorite hymn on a much more than regular basis. My mother about lost her mind. Every time my sisters and I saw the numbers for "Reverently and Meekly Now" on the old wooden board above the organ, we smiled at each other with a leer of excitement, knowing that Que Butterfield had just pushed Mom one step closer to the edge.

Included in this wonderful cadre of people were four of the most amazing yet unassuming widows I've ever met. Small in stature, this stately foursome were spiritual giants who lived the principle of service through example. To those who knew them, Louise Homeke, Myrle Humes, Maude Koyle, and Desna Newman (known as Des) were to the Riverton Second Ward what Frank Sinatra, Dean Martin, Sammy Davis Jr., and Peter Lawford were to the Sands Hotel in Las Vegas. They defined the place.

Maude Koyle was the group's senior stateswoman. When I met her, I felt that knowing a person named Maude had to have some significance in and of itself. An expert in genealogy, she was always busy doing embroidery for others. Her slow cadence and calm demeanor hinted toward the wisdom and dignity borne of a lifetime in the refiner's fire. Maude Koyle never had much to say except for the time that my dad, who later doubled as her bishop, suggested that someone on her meager income did not need to pay fast offerings. In telling the story years later, he never expressed what she said, but the impression was there that she took him to the proverbial woodshed.

Des Newman was a friend to everyone with a quick smile that belied what had to have been sharply honed diplomatic instincts. By the time we hit Riverton, she lived just outside our ward boundaries, an innocent geographic casualty of a decades-old ward split that had rocked the northern end of town. Separated from the sisterhood, Des must have been in a mood to haggle, and so off she went to see the stake president, Leonard Beckstead. While I know of no photographic proof of them coming out of the office smiling and shaking hands, evidence suggests that Des Newman and Leonard Beckstead negotiated an accord. With it came a "special exception" allowing her to attend the old Second Ward. For all the clout that her Henry Kissinger-style tactics seemed to hold, I figured she could have lived in Oslo, Norway, and still have been granted the right to attend the Riverton Second Ward.

Myrle Humes was the foursome's comedian. She loved a good joke and always had a quick comeback. When her humor shifted into overdrive, she slapped her knee and cut loose with her signature laugh. Alternatively, nothing got by Sister Humes. She was shrewd and fearless, and her sweet expression could turn into an I-can-see-right-through-you look before you knew what had happened. Whenever the foursome needed a heavy, she was it. Years later when my dad, as her stake president, made a boundary change that shifted her into a new ward, she walked up to him, looked him in the eye, and said, "Duane, I'm going to come to your house and shoot out the porch light!" Although we didn't think she would follow through, there was no doubt that she could.

The group's fourth member also doubled as one of the chief chauffeurs. It was not a matter of electability as much as it was a matter of logic and necessity. She and Des were the only two who owned cars. And so, Louise Homeke rose to the occasion. She was a slight, adorable, kind woman with a great German accent. She was also the proud owner of an always immaculately clean sky-blue Ford Falcon with a dark-blue interior. Every time I saw that Ford Falcon motoring around town, there were four heads barely visible over the seats. Sister Hoemke drove those women everywhere—visiting, shopping, going to church or the hairdressers—it didn't matter where. If any of them needed anything, there they all went, with Sister Homeke behind the wheel, pushing thirty-five miles per hour in that sky-blue Ford Falcon.

As each Sunday rolled around, Sister Homeke would drive promptly and calmly into the church parking lot in a parking ritual that appeared to move in slow motion. Then these grand ladies helped each other out of the car, walked carefully into the church, and took the same bench in the center of our old illustrious chapel in the same regal manner in which Queen Elizabeth takes her seat at Buckingham Palace. Regardless of the time, everyone left the foursome's bench empty, awaiting their arrival. It was clear to me that everyone knew taking their bench meant answering to Sister Humes.

Humble and giving, they were the epitome of the story of the widow's mite. They flew below the radar in every sense of the word, and yet at the same time, their continual, unsung service made it impossible to miss them. Just like all the Lord's children, these women were not your ordinary quartet. They were women of great faith whose lives and souls had been shaped and molded by what they'd endured and learned along the way. Although I couldn't define my feelings at the time, I now know that I saw their nobility, love, strength, and willingness to endure. They took care of each other, visited around town, and served in the ward wherever they were asked. What most impacted me was how they took the time to serve me. They taught me in classes, they spoke to me in the foyer, they asked me about school—they served me, a young boy of ten years old, by giving me their time.

As we pass through the seasons of our lives, the flurry of opportunities to serve others by simply giving of our time will come from all directions. During those moments, it's difficult to fully comprehend the impact of these simple acts of service. It has been truly humbling to me as I now know how profound the few moments are to me that I spent with a child or a neighbor.

My dad taught me the value of giving of our time when he served as the Second Ward's bishop. Our ward map was heavily populated with elderly couples and widows, and he made sure to visit them all. On many occasions my dad would take me on these visits. A reluctant participant at first, I would sit with him in small living rooms and see how happy these people were to be remembered and visited. They couldn't wait to talk, and I sat in awe of their life's stories, their faith, and their willingness to give. I learned from their life experiences and was strengthened by their devotion to the Lord. Most importantly, I felt the great spirit of service and came to understand the meaning of Matthew 25:40: "Inasmuch as ye have done it unto one of the least of these my brethren, ye have done it unto me."

As we teach our children the great value of service, we enable them to learn one of the great laws of the kingdom—sacrifice. We live in an era that offers the best entertainment, recreation, technology, and consumer products the world has ever seen. These times and amenities offer our children wonderful opportunities. They can also serve as distractions by becoming substitutions for what matters most or vehicles promoting that great con that says you should take care of yourself first. In this environment of prosperity and progress, sacrifice is an increasingly important commodity. And, as in anything, the best way to teach our children to serve is to first do it ourselves. My most impactful lessons on sacrifice and service came from watching what my dad did as opposed to what he said. Further, he never asked me to do anything that he wasn't willing to do himself. When I weeded the garden, he was there with me. When I went to the Church farm, he went with me. Our children don't need us to tell them what they should do as much as they need us to show them.

One of my favorite examples of service in the New Testament is the story of the good Samaritan in Luke 10. Christ shares a parable after being challenged by a lawyer in verses 25–29:

> And behold, a certain lawyer stood up, and tempted him, saying, Master, what shall I do to inherit eternal life? He said unto him, What is written in the law? . . . And he answering said, Thou shalt love the Lord thy God with all thy heart, and with all thy soul, and with all thy strength, and with all thy mind;

> and thy neighbour as thyself. And he said unto him, Thou hast answered right: this do, and thou shalt live. But he, willing to justify himself, said unto Jesus, And who is my neighbour?

In this powerful parable, Jesus teaches who our neighbor is by telling the story of a man who, while traveling a busy yet dangerous road to Jericho, "fell among thieves" (Luke 10:30). Wounded and lying by the side of the road, this man was spotted by two otherwise honorable, believing men. The first, a priest, allowed his fear of additional thieves to justify his decision to pass him by at a safe distance, perhaps on the other side of the road. The second, a Levite, justified his passing with his important place in society and pressing matters that awaited him in Jericho. Surely, both thought, someone would soon follow who would have the time and the courage to help.

The third passerby, however, was the bombshell in the Lord's parable. This man was from Samaria, a place of intercultural marriages where families, part Israelite and part Gentile, were looked down upon and hated by most Jews. This last passerby, a man from a supposed lower class, saw beyond social position and understood not only what it meant to love his neighbor but who his neighbor was. Each time I read this parable, I wonder how often I use excuses to justify myself into passing by on the other side of someone who needs my help.

We pick up the story again in Luke 10:33–37.

> But a certain Samaritan, as he journeyed, came where he was: and when he saw him, he had compassion on him, And went to him, and bound up his wounds, pouring in oil and wine, and set him on his own beast, and brought him to an inn, and took care of him. And on the morrow when he departed, he took out two pence, and gave them to the host, and said unto him, Take care of him; and whatsoever thou spendest more, when I come again, I will repay thee. Which now of these three, thinkest thou, was neighbour unto him that fell among

the thieves? And he said, He that shewed mercy on him. Then said Jesus unto him, Go, and do thou likewise.

Some years ago, as I hurriedly drove along a highway, I pulled to the right shoulder of the road to pass a large excavation truck that I mistakenly assumed was turning left. After it was too late to act, I realized that the driver had swung wide to the left to navigate a difficult right turn, and I drove right into the side of his truck at a high speed. As my car came to a stop after hitting the truck near the back of the cab, I quickly climbed out of the shattered side window. Realizing I had no serious injuries, I recognized that I had experienced a lucky-to-be-alive moment. As I stood somewhat dazed and sore by the side of the road in my suit and tie, awaiting the emergency personnel, I watched people in their cars who looked just like me pass by "on the other side." Adorned in their suits and ties and bearing the marks of otherwise honorable, believing people, I could see their looks of consternation with my act that had backed up traffic for miles. Embarrassed, I couldn't blame them as I knew I'd held that same feeling when coming upon accidents before.

A few moments later my attention was turned to an old, rusty pickup truck that was pulling off the road behind my mangled car. As I watched with surprise, a gaunt, bearded man with old clothes, long hair, and a cigarette in his mouth climbed out of the cab. He walked directly toward me, asked me how I was, and checked me for signs of shock and injury. He helped me clean up, pulled some things from my car, and then stood by my side as if it were the most important place he could be and awaited the arrival of the police and paramedics. Just like the good Samaritan, that man saw me and "had compassion" (Luke 10:33). He "bound up [my] wounds" (Luke 10:34) of embarrassment, shock, and loneliness. He didn't give me oil, wine, or his mount, but he gave me his time and his love until my own "inn" of help and safety could arrive. This man, who I might not have noticed in other settings and who certainly would be looked down upon by some in our society, knew not only what it meant to love his neighbor—he knew his neighbor.

Over the years, I've taken every opportunity to retell this experience to my children as a reminder of what service means, how inconvenient it can be, and how it often comes from people we would never expect it from. One of the important lessons of service is that it's linked to the characteristic of love. With that thought in mind, it's vital that we teach our children how important it is to avoid judging others whose appearance might fall outside established social norms. Service also appears in many forms. It is often planned well in advance, but at other times it requires a split-second decision to run and help. Those quick moments can leave a lasting impression, and so we must prepare ourselves to listen to the Spirit so we recognize those moments when they come.

Talk with your children about how they perceive service. Often, it is the larger, attention-getting projects that come to mind first; however, brainstorming with them will help them see how vast—large or small—the opportunities to serve are. Also, help them learn that in the eyes of the Lord, all service is equal.

A key element of service is action. Even if someone is in need, if you simply ask, most will put on a brave face or be embarrassed and respond that they're okay. The better approach is to seek an impression of what is needed and then just do it. I learned this lesson in a pivotal way from my uncle Glen Markus.

Three years older than my mother, Uncle Glen was born in the middle of the Depression when circumstances were difficult and opportunities minimal. His life in their small family home in Midvale was marked by a meager existence, and yet you would have never known by talking to him. His positive attitude and his joy in serving were a result of his great faith in his Heavenly Father and his understanding that all would work out. His life was all about God and family, and when Uncle Glen spoke of the Lord, you knew that he knew Him. Tall and slender, his countenance radiated patience and goodness, and in his deep-set eyes, you could see his smile and feel his love without him ever speaking a word. When I think of him, I remember a remarkable, kind man who was consistent, always thought of others, and was completely at peace. I challenge each of us to be that kind of man.

When Glen was twenty-two years old, he married Ruth Humes, the daughter of the infamous, aforementioned widow Myrl Humes. They settled in Riverton before we did and raised their five children in a comfortable home where my cousin Kurt and I would lift Eskimo Pies from Aunt Ruth's basement freezer. Life had taught Glen Markus the value of work and making do with what was on hand. He persevered, often working multiple jobs at a time to serve and support his family. Early in his career he worked at the Kennecott Copper Mine in the Oquirrh mountain range on the west side of the Salt Lake Valley. As a brakeman, he rode in the last car of the trains that drove up the mountain and then retreated in reverse to haul away the leftover tailings from the top of the mine back down to the mid-mountain dump.

On one night as the train backed down the hill, all the cars came loose from the engine and headed straight toward the cliff of the dump at breakneck speed. Miraculously, the last car, with Glen inside, became unhitched from the other cars and somehow made the sharp turn in the tracks. As the remaining cars hurtled over the cliff into the dark abyss that was the dump, Glen's car shot down the remainder of the track, came to a standstill, and rocked slightly from side to side at the bottom of the tracks. Clearly, and thankfully, Glen had much more service to render. The Lord, as He always does, saw in Glen what the world did not. Inactive in the Church until after they married, Glen and Ruth Markus became devoted to the Lord, His work, and their family, and the Lord made great use of this uncle of mine. His life was never about pageantry or extravagance. To Glen Markus, the formula for happiness was service, kindness, and simplicity.

He and my Aunt Ruth taught me the power of serving and acting after I received a job following a period of unemployment. Knowing that we only had one car, he called me and told me that he wanted us to use his "spare" Honda until we were able to get a second car. A little prideful and embarrassed, I delayed in picking it up until he called again and told me if I didn't come and get it, he was going to park it in my driveway. That quiet gesture from Glen came at a time when we needed it most. He and Aunt Ruth didn't ask me what I needed; they simply gave what they knew I needed.

A few weeks later, as I was driving home in work traffic, I spotted a stalled truck holding up traffic on I-15. As the traffic snarled behind it, I thought of the kindness of Uncle Glen. I pulled his "spare" Honda off the road and ran up to help this man push his truck to the side of the freeway. Pushing from the driver's side, he looked at me, startled as I opened the passenger door and helped him push. As he looked at me and thanked me, I thought of Glen and his example: Don't ask what you can do, just see the need and do it. To Glen Markus, there was always time to love, always time to serve, and always time to lift others.

Michelle D. Craig, First Counselor in the Young Women General Presidency of The Church of Jesus Christ of Latter-day Saints, taught we should act without delay when receiving promptings. In the October 2019 General Conference she stated, "When you receive promptings and then act with intention, the Lord can use you. The more you act, the more familiar the voice of the Spirit becomes. . . . If you delay, you might forget the prompting or miss the chance to help someone for God."[23] She also encouraged us to get our errand from the Lord. Sister Craig taught, "The prayer Heavenly Father seems eager to answer is our plea to be led to someone who needs our help."[24]

A youth activity that still stands out clearly in my mind is the night when we gathered at Sister Homeke's small home to clean up her yard. After an evening of hard work in her large yard, there stood Sister Homeke on her front porch, looking at us over the top of her sky-blue Ford Falcon parked in the driveway with a smile of gratitude and Christlike love I will never forget.

Those moments of service will create lasting impressions for our children. While serving as a bishop myself, I took one of my sons on a visit to see an elderly couple in our ward. Just like the visits with my dad, my son was treated to rich conversation and a lesson on service. As we drove away from their home, my son Matthew told me he had a strange feeling. When I pressed for his thoughts, he responded that during our visit he felt so happy he wanted to cry. Suddenly I felt the same way. As we talked about the great lessons of service, I quietly thanked my Heavenly Father for providing my son with a valuable lesson. And I quietly thanked my dad for taking me, the reluctant participant, on the same journey so many years before.

––––– 6 –––––

The Red Sox, the Yankees, and Dad's Back Lawn

Lessons on Priorities

"A surreal feeling rested in my soul as I wandered, like a stranger in a strange land, back to the dugout."

My conversion date was October 22, 1975. Of course, I'm referring to my boyhood conversion to the Boston Red Sox. I had already considered the Red Sox for my favorite team and was nearly convinced while watching a replay of a particularly close game on the old NBC "Saturday Game of the Week" on television a few years before. On a sunny summer afternoon, popular Red Sox left fielder and first baseman, Carl Yastrzemski, singled straight up the middle to center field. Within a few seconds, Yastrzemski jumped off first base as the next hitter ripped a line drive, fair by inches, down the right field line. He gracefully rounded second, sprinted toward third, and was animatedly waved home by the third base coach. My heart raced and chills went up and down my spine as Yastrzemski slid home in a cloud of beautiful brown dust—just ahead of the throw from right field and the tag by the catcher. The home plate umpire leaned directly over the diving catcher, flinging his arms out to his sides to signal the safe call, and I knew I'd seen something of beauty. It was my first exposure to real art.

However, as any kid will tell you, sports conversions typically come as something of a magical moment—an epiphany, if you will. And so it was for me and the Red Sox one fateful October night in game six of the 1975 World Series.

The Cincinnati Reds and their Big Red Machine of the 1970s came into the game leading the Red Sox three games to two. As a result, game six at Boston's fabled Fenway Park was do-or-die for the Boston Red Sox. Trailing 6 to 3, the drama began to unfold when Red Sox pinch hitter Bernie Carbo launched a three-run home run into the center field seats to tie the score in the bottom of the eighth. As the ninth inning passed without a run, the game moved into extra innings, and the stage was set for what would be christened one of the greatest games in World Series history.

With the score still tied at 6 to 6, Red Sox catcher Carlton Fisk walked to the plate just past 12:30 a.m. to lead off the bottom of the twelfth inning. Fisk stepped into the batter's box, facing Cincinnati relief pitcher Pat Darcy before a sellout crowd waiting to erupt. The first pitch, a ball, was followed by a low sinker. With a perfect-for-the-ages swing, Fisk hit a towering fly ball toward the left field foul pole and the lights over Fenway Park's legendary left field wall known as the Green Monster. The crowd roared and everything seemed to move in slow motion as the ball flew through the crisp, autumn New England night. As the ball soared up and out, it appeared to be headed for foul territory. Fisk watched the ball in the air and, taking a couple of steps toward first base, waved both arms three times toward fair territory as if he had the power to control the wind.[25] Sheer pandemonium erupted and Fisk jumped all the way to first base as the ball grazed the foul pole—fair by inches—and flew over the wall, off the screen above the Green Monster, into history, and into my heart. With one now-famous swing, the Red Sox had tied the Series. And even though the Red Sox lost the Series in game seven, my epiphany was complete: I was an official Red Sox fan. To this day, I still see Fisk in my mind, dancing toward first base, waving that ball fair.

My dad, on the other hand, was a New York Yankees fan. Anyone who knows of the heated Yankee–Red Sox rivalry knows the profound significance of that statement. Nothing more can really be said. But there was no malice on my part, no desire to go against the grain; it was one magical swing by a catcher named Carlton Fisk. To my dad's credit, he gracefully accepted my position. Who knows how these things happen, but I'm sure my dad wondered where he went wrong. He did seem more vigilant about my upbringing after that.

Rivalry aside, it was my dad who first endowed me with the love of baseball. He was my first hero. A good ballplayer in his own right, he threw me my first ball and was my first little league coach. He grew up listening to the Yankees on the radio from tiny Castle Dale, Utah, and was raised on a strict diet of players like Joe DiMaggio, Yogi Berra, Whitey Ford, Mickey Mantle, and the great Yankee teams of the late 1940s and 1950s. With those great lineups, who could blame him for being a Yankee fan? He always told me that the feuding Yankees of the late 1970s soured him, but I knew, deep in his heart, dad was still a Yank.

I loved baseball and watched and thought about it constantly. From the time I first learned to catch, I looked forward to the day when I could play little league ball. Finally, when that day came, dad ceremoniously signed me up to play in Riverton's little league and volunteered to be my team's coach. Waiting for the season to begin, I wandered around the house telling anyone who would listen that my home run swing was at its peak. The time had truly come for me to take my place among the greats.

The season opener finally arrived after weeks of practice. I approached my first game with great anticipation and knew that my first ever time at bat would result in a breathtaking, change-the-outcome-of-the-game home run. As I slowly, yet confidently, walked toward home plate in that historic moment, I saw the whole scene unfold in my mind. I was about to redefine the term *long ball*. Standing at the plate, I did what I'd seen every major league hitter do on television: I hit my spikes with the bat, tilted my batting helmet, took my place in the batter's box, and took a couple of obligatory practice swings. As I eyed the field, I determined that a blast to straightaway center field offered the greatest impact. The moment, frozen in time, unfolded as the pitcher began his windup. I clenched my jaw, squared my shoulders, slightly waved the end of my bat above my head and . . . looked at three pitches. All strikes. The bat never left my shoulder. After the umpire called the third strike, a surreal feeling rested in my soul as I wandered, like a stranger in a strange land, back to the dugout. Stunned and devastated, I began to panic as I realized I may have had the shortest time at bat in the history of Riverton little league baseball. To add insult to injury, over the course of the game I also found out my throwing arm wasn't what I'd thought it was. It suddenly dawned on me why I'd been marooned in right field.

On the long ride home, my dad did what he has always done after my disappointments: he lifted me up. Just as he always has, he saw a great opportunity to teach. As fathers, we will be witnesses to our children's experiences in both success and failure. Some of life's greatest character-building lessons come through achievements in victory as well as grace in defeat. On that summer afternoon, my dad reminded me that Babe Ruth's 714 career home runs overshadowed his 1,330 strikeouts, and he helped me understand that character comes from both success and failure. The secret wasn't in not failing; the secret was in getting back up after having failed. He taught me that the people who achieve great things are those who accept failure and come back with a determination to work harder and keep trying. I learned that greatness required more than dreaming: it required work and determination. When asked how he dealt with failure, Paul Harvey, the famed radio commentator, simply stated, "I just get up again when I fall down."[26] In the back seat of our car, I perked up, held on to my dream, and determined to get back up.

At home, I went in solitude to our backyard and faced the imposing brick wall of the back of our garage. Our garage was connected to the end of our house with a raised cement patio that separated it from the expanse of our back lawn. It was here where I would become a baseball player. Day after day, week after week, month after month, and year after year I threw balls at that brick wall under sunshine, shade, clouds, rain, and even snow.

Each February I reported for spring training, and I played on my field of dreams through the World Series in October. I learned to pitch off the wall and field ground balls off the patio. I knew that wall so well that I knew which bricks, when hit exactly right, would produce a fly ball.

Over the years I played countless full-length games and created my own fantasy leagues long before they were in vogue. I memorized statistics, replayed history, and learned the ins and outs of America's pastime. Throwing against that brick wall became more than practice. It was therapeutic; it was a place where I witnessed my own improvement, and it was a symbol of my happy childhood. It was also the place where my dad—through action, not word—taught me about priorities.

The spot on the lawn where I threw from quickly succumbed to my daily baseball battery. The remaining dirt sunk a few inches and hardened. The better I became, the farther I stood from the garage wall, expanding my "pitcher's mound" to roughly fifteen feet long by five feet wide. Over the course of a few weeks, dad's beautiful green oasis developed a stark, parched sinkhole that looked like an industrial holding pond during rainstorms. But through it all, my dad never said a word. Regardless of the horror expressed by many ("Duane, what happened to your lawn?!"), he simply smiled and watched me play. My dad knew how important it was to me. He not only knew that I wanted to become a better baseball player—he wanted to let me learn how to persevere. Through it all, I became a better baseball player. But more importantly, my dad taught me about priorities as I learned what his were. He showed me that I was far more important to him than a nicely groomed back lawn.

One of a father's greatest challenges in life is to juggle the many responsibilities that come his way. We are husbands, fathers, sons, and brothers. We build a career so we can provide for our family's many needs, and we plan time to provide them with life's opportunities. When we add service in our communities and churches, as well as regular daily obligations, our lives can become remarkably busy. However, what really matters to us will certainly be noticed by our children. As I grew up, I learned what was important by observing what was important to my dad. Despite my father's many responsibilities, he always made sure that my mother, my brothers, my sisters, and I came first. Whether it was a ball game or dance recital, a concert or simple one-on-one conversation, he would sacrifice any kind of personal success or leisure time to be there. I don't know that I've ever known anyone who had a firmer understanding of priorities.

Field of Dreams, a hit movie in the 1980s (based on W.P. Kinsella's 1982 novel *Shoeless Joe*), tells the story of an Iowa farmer named Ray Kinsella who, after hearing a voice from his cornfield whispering, "If you build it, they will come," plows up part of his corn fields and constructs a beautiful baseball field. Within a short time, baseball players from days gone by, led by Shoeless Joe Jackson and his teammates from the famed 1919 Chicago White Sox who accepted money to throw the World Series. Seeking to relive their dreams, they ask for permission to play on Ray's field.

However, as Ray joyfully watches these players from the past, the looming question remains: is there a purpose or a dream for him? The climax to the story occurs when Shoeless Joe Jackson, standing in the outfield with Ray, points back toward the field and says "Ray, if you build it, he will come." Turning his gaze back toward the infield, Ray sees one last player standing and waiting for him at home plate. In a moving moment that should stir the nostalgia in any father or son, Ray approaches this young minor league catcher only to suddenly realize that it's his own deceased father as a young man. In this powerful scene, Ray finally realizes his dream in his own backyard as he says, "Dad, do you want to have a catch?" Ray's dream was simply to be close to his dad.[27]

That closing scene has so much meaning and so many messages in that one small round of catch. We search the world over for success, adventure, possessions, and experiences that will remind the world of our importance. And yet, as we search for seeming greatness, we risk missing the greatest events of all—those simple acts and precious moments with those whose lives most benefit from our attention and love. We often miss the mark by losing sight of the people and relationships that matter most.

Time and time again I find, just as my dad taught me, that my top priorities are right in my own backyard. They are little people who grow up too fast. They make messes, they always want to wrestle, and they create a great deal of work. The beauty of them is that they're not yet jaded by the world and all its false gods. They're happy, and their greatest satisfaction is found in a proverbial game of catch.

I recall a moment when my youngest daughter insisted on helping me do some work outside. I've always been amazed when the youngest who can help the least insists on helping while those who can help the most become masters of illusion. But work together we did. She laughed and smiled from ear to ear as we talked and as she performed the small tasks I gave her. One of my greatest thrills came as my three-year-old daughter looked at me and said, "Dad, do you know how much I love you?"

I looked at my precious little girl and said, "I do; do you know how much I love you?"

"I do, Daddy," she said. In my world of priorities that day, Eliza knew where she fit. The contributions we make in our children's lives are moments of greatness that, although unknown to the world, offer the most profound and lasting impact. Our children as they grow, our parents as they age, our wives as they stand by us—are there any better marks of importance?

When I first began my career in banking, I rose quickly and achieved a measure of success. I also became involved politically and was given the opportunity to serve on many community boards and commissions. I was a busy man with many obligations, and the world told me that, because I was busy and had many responsibilities, I was important and successful. My endeavors had worth, and it all seemed so exciting. I was becoming well-known and respected, and it fueled my desire for more. Later I was offered a position as a CEO of an organization where I thought I could really leave a lasting imprint. I put every ounce of energy I had into it and worked hard to enhance and build what I'd been given.

One day at the conclusion of an important meeting, I picked up my cell phone to play the messages that had been left. The last message was profound and led me to some re-evaluation. My oldest son, Matthew, in his excited third-grade voice, told me that he'd swept the gymnasium and cafeteria at school and, as a reward, had been given two small Butterfinger candy bars. He ate one and then, knowing that I love Butterfingers, was calling to tell me what he had done and that he was saving the other Butterfinger for me. Tears welled up in my eyes as I smiled and remembered what was most important in my life. Many things occupied my mind on that day. Of all those that occupied my son's mind, nothing had pushed me out of the forefront of it.

Years later I look back on that time with different eyes. That CEO position is now in the past; it was a great learning experience although I didn't accomplish all I hoped to. The board assignments have come and gone, and I've achieved success and experienced failure. Throughout these experiences, my stock, just like others who succeed and fail, has risen and fallen with the tides. The true tests in life come when, amid failure or trial, we remember who we are, what really matters, and how to get back up. Those who are the most important to us are those who stand with us during our hardest times. Regardless of what does or does not come, when the dust settles, it is our Heavenly Father, the Savior, true friends, and our families who are still there. And so, we should be with them also. I can't remember who I was meeting with, the topic of the meeting, or one other thing I was doing or worrying about on the day Matthew called me about the candy bar. But I'll never forget his words, the sound of his voice, his pride for having done something good, and his excitement to tell me what he had for me. Time marches on, but Matthew and I still love Butterfingers.

As I think back on that voicemail message from Matthew, as well as countless other bits of exciting news and important requests from my other children, it brings to light the story from chapter 3. You'll recall that Elder J. Devn Cornish told of his simple prayer that was heard and answered by a loving Heavenly Father who, despite the unimaginable enormity of who He is, made a young father on a sidewalk in Boston a priority. As fathers, we should strive to obtain that great characteristic when dealing with our children. In their less busy and less complex lives, surely there are events to attend and stories to tell that mean a great deal to them but can be lost or ignored by us. I am not perfect; however, I try each day to stop and pay attention so that what matters to them does indeed matter to me.

One of life's most important roles is that of leadership in the family. There are certainly cases where divorce or single-parent families exist, and many determined, loving individuals in those situations give their all for their children and enable them to succeed. However, the ideal laboratory for a child's education, conduct, development, and success is found within a family. Community programs, schools, society, or friends are ineffective substitutes for a father and mother—the love and teaching that come from them can't be replicated.

It has often been said "When you're with your wife, be with your wife. When you're with your children, be with your children." In other words, a physical presence alone is a poor substitute for full engagement. We need to be engaged in whatever we're doing with our wives and children. There is no cell phone call, no text message, no video game, no meeting, no activity that is more important than the impact we have as patriarchs fulfilling our greatest role in mortality.

Another place where we should direct our priorities is to our Heavenly Father and His Only Begotten Son. The blessings that come when we establish a priority of worship and gospel teaching in our homes impact generations. It isn't enough to do those things that are publicly seen. The development of a close, personal relationship with deity and the practices that enable it should always be a top priority. When a father lives and conducts himself through principles of faith and a commitment to God, he will bless all those within his influence. That is where the richer, deeper, and fuller life is found. When our hearts leave the things of the world for the things of eternity, our hearts are at peace. The marked difference between the priorities that the world teaches versus the priorities that the Lord teaches is found in a stirring story of faith and testimony in I Kings 18.

In approximately 922 BC, the house of Israel, rife with discord, split into two kingdoms. Since the days of Jacob, rivalries had existed between Jacob's sons, and tensions among the tribes continued and intensified through history. King Solomon saw increased unrest during his reign, particularly when he learned that Jeroboam, the man he had placed in charge of the tribes of Ephraim and Manasseh, had been told by the prophet Ahijah that he would become ruler over ten of the twelve tribes. Fearful of Jeroboam, Solomon decided to get rid of him for good.

Meanwhile, knowing of the Lord's frustration with the growing worldliness of His chosen people, Ahijah counseled Jeroboam to follow the path of the Lord. At that moment, however, Jeroboam was more concerned about Solomon's increasing wrath, and so off he went to Egypt to await the death of the king.

When Solomon passed away and his son Rehoboam took over, people from the north called on Jeroboam to return and lead them against him. When Jeroboam and his group were refused by Rehoboam in their attempt to seek tax relief from the heavy burdens placed on them by Solomon, the spark that would end a united Israel was ignited. The house of Israel split, with the ten tribes settling what came to be known as Israel in the north while the tribes of Judah and Benjamin stayed in Judah in the south.

Unfortunately, Jeroboam wasn't exact in following the Lord's instructions, and it wasn't long before idol worship came back in vogue in the northern kingdom. As the years passed, Israel in the north became increasingly concerned about foreign enemies. In what might have been viewed at the time as a stroke of political brilliance, King Ahab, who ruled about fifty years after Jeroboam, determined that a political alliance with Phoenicia to the north (modern-day Lebanon) would help subdue thoughts of invasion by foreign powers. As a result, a royal wedding was held, and King Ahab married a glamorous Phoenician princess named Jezebel.

Jezebel, accustomed to the vast diversity of her homeland, brought along her religious beliefs that consisted of the worship of a god known as Baal. Over time, her power and influence grew. She sent home for prophets of Baal to join her, and she instituted the worship of her god among the people of Israel. In a fit of rage directed at those who taught against her, Jezebel ordered the execution of some of Israel's prophets. Amid this din of violence, the Lord sent Elijah the prophet, who promptly strode into town, commanded a drought, and then, heeding the voice of the Lord, went into hiding.

After some time, the Lord commanded the restless Elijah to return and show Jezebel and a faithless people the power of God by ending the drought. Elijah called upon God for guidance and support and then challenged the false prophets of Baal to a biblical duel of power from on high to bring about the end of the long drought. After multiple failed attempts by Jezebel's prophets, Elijah's appeal to God was answered in a stunning display as rains poured from the heavens and soaked the parched earth. The audacious, worldly rituals of these followers of Satan were no match for the overwhelming, torrential power of Almighty God. And when it came to their spokespersons, the arrogant, ignorant prophets of Baal were reduced to complete insignificance by the humble yet powerful Elijah. Elijah's formula of calling upon God in humility, speaking His word, and showing forth God's power has never failed the faithful followers of the Lord.

In the final act of showing God's power, Elijah asked the people, "How long halt ye between two opinions? if the Lord be God, follow him: but if Baal, then follow him. And the people answered him not a word" (1 Kings 18:21). Too attached to the world, the halted position of the citizens of Israel would not allow an uttered word. How often do we halt between opinions or hesitate in completely committing to the one true and living God? How often do we halt with our priorities and justify our focus on the things which matter least? The answer is simple: "If the Lord be God, follow him: but if Baal [or the world], then follow him."

Great will be the legacy of the father who simply follows God. In my dad's life, his Lord is God, and he's always followed Him. My little league experience, like everything else under his tutelage, was much more than fundamentals and rules. Regardless of the circumstance, his actions were the same. Life was about learning and growing, doing your absolute best, and treating others with love and respect. It was about striving to become like the Savior and remembering to put God and family first.

In every conversation I've had with someone in the twilight of their lives, they've said nothing of careers, awards, wealth, or possessions. It has always been family—the people, the events, the memories. Each time a loved one passes away, we're reminded of priorities. Left behind in this imperfect world are their possessions, their homes, and their careers. Those things they take with them on their journey back are those things that matter to God—the impact they had on others, the offerings they made, the knowledge they gained, the characteristics they developed, and their faith in the promises of eternal glory.

As the years progressed, our backyard remained largely the same. A few trees were pulled down and a small white fence sprouted around a flower garden and birdbath, but the garage and patio remained in their proper place, and I was always able to get a fly ball off them. The fifteen by five sinkhole remained, although the grass did finally grow back. When I left home for a church mission, my mom suggested to my dad that he could finally have his lawn back. As he gazed through the window into the backyard, he told her he wanted to leave it as it was. I guess it represented a great deal to the both of us. It was a place where dreams were fulfilled and where dad taught me what really mattered.

One summer several years ago, our extended family went on an outing together. My sons and I, as we always do, threw our baseball gloves, a bat, and a ball in the back of the car before leaving home. After a picnic in a park, I picked up one of my son's gloves and tossed it to my dad. There we stood, a forty-year-old son playing catch with his seventy-year-old dad, with my own sons, grinning ear to ear, sitting on the grass watching us. I might as well have been ten again throwing to my young father, for the feeling and thrill were still the same.

In 1941, Grantland Rice, an influential sportswriter from the early to mid-1900s, wrote a verse fitting for both sports and life. It perfectly describes the great man who is my father as well as the greatest lesson he ever taught me about focusing on what matters most. The illustrious Rice wrote:

For when the One Great Scorer comes to mark against your name,
He writes—not that you won or lost—but how you played the Game.[28]

— 7 —

The Journey Is the Destination

Lessons on Gratitude

"You're sitting on my coils."

Right in the middle of the Salt Lake Valley rests a community aptly named Midvale. Established in the early 1850s by pioneers from The Church of Jesus Christ of Latter-day Saints, it developed a diverse economy based on agriculture, mining, and milling. By the 1870s, Bingham Junction, as it was called, had become the midpoint for the railroads between mining in Little Cottonwood Canyon to the east and Bingham Canyon to the west. The community boomed and became a melting pot for farmers, laborers, and immigrant miners.

My mother was born in a humble neighborhood in Midvale's old downtown district, where her family of nine lived in a small two-bedroom house flanked by Main Street to the west and the railroad tracks to the east. One of the greatest lessons my mother learned from her humble upbringing was gratitude. Her family simply never had much in the way of material things. The Great Depression didn't make things any easier, and it took its toll on the Max and Jennie Markus family. Not a Christmas season goes by without my thinking of one of my mother's Christmas mornings from the 1940s. She and her younger sister, both excited little girls, awoke to find a small new table with two new robes draped over its sides. Underneath the robes on the table's bottom shelf sat their only other present: a small toy cash register to share. I think not only of their disappointment but also of the heartache that my grandparents had to have felt.

But among life's disappointments, my mother learned gratitude. Her parents loved her, and they always had food to eat and clothes to wear, and they learned how to be grateful and how to give. And laced within that humble chemistry was a brand of humor that today would have spawned reality television. They knew that the best antidote for anything was laughter, and the Markus family was loaded with it. My grandfather's humor was in-your-face hilarity with the occasional colorful word while my grandmother's was so subtle that you didn't recognize it until it was a block away in the other direction. This combination of character traits developed in them a unique perspective when looking at the world.

It was this interesting combination that developed my mother's outlook on life. Full of heart, she always believed in us and encouraged us to look out for the underdog—probably because she'd always felt like one. She would give you the shirt off her back but deliver a verbal George Foreman–type roundhouse if you backed her into a corner. To top it all, she was blessed with both brands of humor that her parents possessed, giving her a legendary, out-of-left-field sense of humor which provided the perfect remedy for anything that ailed you. If I hadn't known better, I would've sworn she did two shows a night in Las Vegas.

The queen of perfect timing, it wasn't just slapstick and one-liners that stole the limelight. Her brand of humor had strength of narrative and a subtle sense of wisdom and irony that spewed forth a statement for any predicament. Two parts Plato, three parts Mother Theresa, three parts stand-up comedian, and two parts longshoreman, she could wax poetic or smatter nuances with the wit and sarcasm of a seafaring man. Needless to say, my siblings and I knew we were being raised by one of the great philosophers of our time.

Her environment also instilled a sense of determination that was evident in everything she did—from the way she protected us to the way she drove. I recall one instance during a wild ride to downtown Salt Lake in my dad's old pickup truck. We were late, and she was rattled and intent on making up for lost time with the element of speed. All I remember is her clenched mouth telling us to keep quiet as she approached the railroad tracks in Riverton in the same manner that Patton advanced on Germany. Not anticipating the height of the approaching rise in the road, Mom hit a small swell of air as she hit the tracks, and I sat there just hoping she could shift the old Chevy into fourth. You could have cut the tension in the cab with a knife. Barely audible, I heard what seemed to be my sister Sharon's first attempt at reciting the Lord's Prayer.

As I grew into my teenage years and passed through college, I developed the habit of going into my parents' room as they were going to bed to talk about the day, school, girls, life, or whatever else was on my mind. My siblings followed suit, and before long, their bedroom was crowded with conversationalists. During one of those sessions on a cold winter night, my mother climbed into bed and pulled her beloved electric blanket over her. As I sat down on the bed to continue the dialogue, she pointed to her electric blanket and calmly stated, "You're sitting on my coils." From that time on, we referred to those nighttime chats as "sitting on the coils."

Those late-night conversations were a vital part of my communication with my parents. In that relaxed setting, the humor flew at full strength, and my dad lay by Mom's side just quietly chuckling. We knew we could talk about anything, and we knew their time was ours. Theodore Roosevelt, the twenty-sixth president of the United States, once said, "Nine-tenths of wisdom consists in being wise in time."[29] A precious commodity, time is one thing we can't buy, and I came to be grateful for it.

Time spent with our children and time listening to our children can be among the greatest gifts we give them. We all come with different abilities and different styles when it comes to communication. The key is to understand that your children will treasure any time you give them and any attempts at communication you provide. Be yourself and love them, and they will cherish those moments with you. What they crave is your attention, your acceptance, and your encouragement. My own experience has taught me to watch for that inevitable clash of time, as the moments when my children seem the most discussion-prone are when I'm the least. Don't miss out on those moments when they become conversationalists as you're rushing them to school, dashing through the grocery store, or putting them to bed. What may seem inopportune when you're tired and rushed can become priceless if you can take a breath, slow down, and listen.

Of the many lessons I've learned from my own children, one that stands out has been their gratitude for time. It hasn't only been well-planned events that have brought them joy. It's most often simply been time with us and time together.

One day many years ago, JoAnn took our son Stephen, then four years old, to a quaint shopping village where a mother duck and her ducklings were swimming around a small pond. As they crossed a covered bridge to watch, Stephen looked at his mother and said, "Mom, wouldn't it be great if I was that duck, and you were my duck mom?" Stephen loved that time with her, and even in his little boy imagination didn't want to be without his mother.

Remember, in terms of spending time with your children, quality is as important as quantity. Again, when you're with them, be with them. We have too many things that can distract us from quality time. If we spend a whole day with our children but spend part of it on our cell phone, we've missed the boat.

During the years when we're raising our children, we seem to have the most things competing for our time. We're too easily distracted by the cares of the world and fall into the belief that we must give our children everything and give them every opportunity to discover what the world can offer them. Often the best thing we can do is sit back and see the world through the eyes of our children, where there is magic in everything new and awe in life's simple pleasures.

When our daughter Julee was in first grade, she wrote an entry in her school journal saying that I'd brought her a candy bar and how happy that gesture had made her. Later, in her early teenage years, she let me see a portion of her journal about our trip to Disneyland. Of everything she noted, the most detail was given to a fifteen-minute period when just she and I talked together on our way to buy Disney's famous churros. There we were, smack-dab in the middle of Disneyland, and yet what she loved most was the one-on-one time with me. Despite their protests, our children want to be with us. Further, I've found they don't expect perfection. They just want a father who loves them and loves to be around them.

Several years ago, my wife and I took our children on a trip to the United States' eastern seaboard to visit American and church history sights—not to mention a pilgrimage to Fenway Park to watch our beloved Boston Red Sox. We'd masterfully planned every minute of the trip and finally flew from Salt Lake to Washington, D.C. full of excitement for all that our children would see and experience.

On day two of our excursion, we jumped on one of Washington, D.C.'s metro trains from our hotel in Alexandria, Virginia, for a trip into D.C. After boarding the train, I watched my four-and-a-half-year-old daughter Emma carefully study the train and its movement. She smiled at me broadly, letting me know she was enjoying this simple pleasure of our trip. Then, with all the eloquence she could muster, she stated, "Actually Dad, between the plane and the train, I think the plane is faster." Unfazed by the magnitude of the trip, Emma reminded me that soaking in and enjoying every moment was the prize of gratitude.

As we've spent time traveling with our children, their common answer to the question "What was your favorite part of the trip?" has been "Being with family." Through nostalgic eyes, my longing for the simpler days of the past has enabled me to bask in the moments with our children—nights spent looking at the numerous stars or days spent drinking lemonade on the mound obscured by scrub oak in our front yard. Time and time again we hear stories of people who thought they had everything but then found that, without time with loved ones, they had nothing. It's the simple things that last, and our losses are ever so poignant when we realize time is something we can't bring back.

As my wait to become a father waned on, I observed as best I could everything about fatherhood. One of the best lessons I learned from that wait was that little children grow up fast. Although I knew I would never be perfect, I committed to never put off trying to be a good, engaged father.

When our three oldest sons were young, we began the tradition of having pizza and watching movies on Friday nights. On one late Friday night, I sat on the floor by Johnathan, watching *The Son of Flubber*, while his brothers and my wife slept on the couch. As he sat excitedly watching a football game scene, unable to hold in his emotions, he jumped up and yelled, "Great game!" Then, he hit middle school, slid through high school, stormed through a mission, and went to college. It seemed like he grew up overnight. The quick passage of time makes that moment with Johnathan, along with so many just like it, the treasures of my life.

Those Friday nights became one of the best investments we ever made with a return that I could never have imagined. And after all these years, I still look forward to them when we sit down with the blankets, popcorn, and cookies with our younger children. These simple pleasures are part of what President Thomas S. Monson meant when he said, "find joy in the journey—now."[30] Along with these journeys come the more mundane moments of life. Daily living brings sleepless nights, countless diapers, sinks full of dishes, half-empty toolboxes, and laundry room floors covered with laundry, some of which you'll swear you saw waiting to be folded yesterday. Just remember, all too soon, the day will come when one load of laundry will do the trick and you'll long for the days when it took three months to find your large screwdriver.

Often, these simple moments come completely out of the blue. On one particularly hectic day, I ran to the grocery store with my three little girls. As we left the grocery store, they begged me to let them ride a miniature merry-go-round that sat in front of the store. With my mind full of thoughts relative to chores, work, and other supposedly pressing matters, I responded, "We'll ride it next time, girls." As I loaded them into the car, they reminded me that I'd told them the same thing the last time they'd asked. At that same moment, a car pulled in next to mine, and three teenaged girls jumped out and walked into the store. I turned and looked at my daughters' sweet faces and remembered that my little girls wouldn't be little forever. To squeals of delight, I said, "Let's go!" I got them back out of the car, and we ran to the miniature merry-go-round. As I watched them laughing and waving to me as they rode tiny plastic horses in a small circle, I was grateful for the joy that such small and simple pleasures can bring a child. A five-minute delay became instant and lasting joy for them and for me, and I quickly realized how unimportant some things are and how especially important little things are. I look back today, so grateful that I followed a prompting to take advantage of that moment as my girls, now aged eighteen, seventeen, and fifteen, are no longer interested in miniature merry-go-rounds.

Nowhere in our lives is time as important as it is in our relationship with our Heavenly Father. His way is to have time for reflection, time to draw close to Him, and time to do good. His most ardent desire is that we take time with our Creator so we may come to know Him. When we spend time reflecting and pondering our relationship with Him, we draw closer to Him, better understand our purpose, and receive the guidance we need to follow the path He would have us take. Certainly, we're far better served when we follow the path He has for us as opposed to a path we might take without His guidance.

An additional benefit to taking the time to think about Him is we come to see that all we have is because of Him. We see His hands in every part of our lives and become more grateful to Him for what we have.

At a time of financial difficulty in our family, we were grateful for a lesson our son taught us. One night during our family prayer, he asked the Lord to "help us be grateful for what we have and not worry about what we don't have." It's important that we look past the fleeting happiness of "things" and have gratitude for the details of our lives—family, gospel truths, freedom, health, the earth, and all things that were created for our joy and benefit. A friend of mine reminded me of this when he taught how we often thank our Heavenly Father for the boat when perhaps our Father's reply might be, "Yes, but what about the lake?"

Gratitude then becomes an exercise in feeling positive. Reflecting on what we have helps us forget about what we don't have. Further, it helps us see what is important and helps move the focus of our thinking away from the challenges of our lives and the worries of the world. If all we think about are the things that are wrong with our lives, it becomes difficult to allow positive thoughts in our minds that develop faith, enlightenment, energy, and solutions. I've often been reminded to enjoy the deeper, richer, fuller life. As I've walked through my ongoing journey in fatherhood, I've come to see that this phrase pertains to those lessons that matter most. Surely the peace that comes from knowing and following God brings about a deeper, richer, fuller life.

While sitting in a major U.S. airport a few years ago, I became fascinated as I observed the countless number of people passing my gate area.

Whether they were arriving, departing, or changing planes, each wore varying looks of urgency, worry, fatigue, or excitement. They came in all sizes, shapes, and nationalities, and all were intent on their own business, seemingly unaware of the mass of humanity that surrounded them.

In those moments of observation, I began to wonder who they were, where they lived, where they were headed, and what their life circumstances were. In each face, I recognized what I often feel. Despite our many differences, each of God's children is so much alike. We want to find happiness, we want to enjoy life, we want the best for our families, and we worry about the future. We just allow the cares of our lives to govern our time and dictate our priorities. We allow the noise of the world to drown out the reflections that our Heavenly Father wants us to have.

In 2013, The Church of Jesus Christ of Latter-day Saints created a video through its Mormon Channel entitled "Earthly Father, Heavenly Father." It examines an earthly father's observations of his own children as he arises early each morning and observes them as they "lie in their beds, unaware" that he is watching. It notes how this man's children explore, play, and eat, unaware of what their father provides them. This earthly father works away from home and yet is close, always thinking of them. In the dialogue, he states of his children, "They see so little of how it all came to be, never questioning, only trusting."[31]

Counted among life's many blessings is how our Heavenly Father utilizes parenthood to give us a glimpse into how He feels about all His children. When I think about and watch our children, my love for them and gratitude for them are beyond my ability to put into words, and I come to see in an exceedingly small way how my Father in Heaven feels about His children. This great plan of salvation, authored by our Heavenly Father at our request, was designed to give us what we asked Him for: the ability to become like Him. As such, it requires us to experience both ends of life's spectrum—health and sickness, pleasure and disappointment, happiness and sadness, ease and adversity, success and failure, triumph and defeat.

However, through it all, He is there—far away and yet so close to lift us, to strengthen us, and to answer even our simplest prayers.

This thought was reinforced one day as JoAnn and I watched a young father walking along the side of a lake with his small daughter. As she walked closer to the water, without her knowing why, the father moved between his daughter and the water to keep her safe from a danger she didn't recognize. And so it is with our Father in Heaven. He protects us from dangers that are unknown by providing the constant companionship of the Holy Ghost to all who qualify for it. From His throne on high, He sees every aspect of our lives and is always seeking to walk between us and the water.

As I sat away from home in that airport, alone in a sea of people, I wondered how many of us are aware of how it all came to be. The earth is abundant with seeds that sprout vegetables and fruits while the beauties of the world enhance our existence and bring joy to our lives. The bright sun lights our days and warms our bodies while the stars in the sky illuminate our nights and give us a glimpse of the vastness of the universe. He has given us a beautiful world and all we need to sustain ourselves. In addition, He has given us gospel knowledge and truth as well as His Only Begotten Son to enable the great plan. When I remember all this, my heart is full of gratitude, and in those moments of reflection, I feel a great obligation to teach my children the great lesson of gratitude.

At the close of the "Earthly Father, Heavenly Father" video, the earthly father, aware of what he has been given and understanding the parallel between being a father on earth and a father in heaven, states, "I am a father. I am also a son. And while I may not understand all that He does for me, I do know that all that I am and all that I have is because He is a father to me. I now stand, very aware of how it all came to be."[32] In my role as a father, not a day goes by when I don't reflect on how grateful I am for my Heavenly Father, for how grateful I am to be a father, and for how very aware I am of how it all came to be.

— 8 —

City Beautiful

Lessons on Adversity

*"My son, peace be unto thy soul; thine adversity and
thine afflictions shall be but a small moment."*

Some 940 miles from its headwaters in Minnesota and just under 1,400 miles from New Orleans to the south, the great Mississippi River turns west and then gently to the southwest at Fort Madison, Iowa. Just a few miles farther south, the river wraps around a distinct, green, fertile swath of Illinois that juts into its path before turning southeast and then south again on its way to St. Louis. About three-quarters of a mile east of the river, this fertile piece of land slopes dramatically up to a bluff where a commanding view of the Mississippi River and Iowa beyond lies to the west while thousands of acres of fertile Illinois farmland lie to the east. Early settlers of the area saw this riverside spot's commercial potential, and by the mid-1830s a small community, aptly called Commerce, sat at the river's bend.[33]

During the infancy of the United States, the mighty Mississippi formed the nation's western border and served as a major transportation route as people and goods moved through the nation's developing waterways.[34] When Thomas Jefferson began his first term as the United States' third president, Napoleon was wringing his hands across the Atlantic in France. A failure to put down a rebellion in their Caribbean colony of Saint-Domingue (present-day Haiti) combined with concerns of a potential war with Great Britain found Napoleon looking around for extra cash to fund his military. In what would become one of history's greatest land grabs, Jefferson recognized opportunity when he saw it and bought 530,000,000 acres of land from the French for a cool $15 million in a deal dubbed the Louisiana Purchase.[35]

Suddenly, the United States and its territories spread west and northwest beyond the Mississippi River, covering what would become seven complete states and parts of eight others. With the Revolution behind them and millions of acres to discover to the west, the America of the early 1800s seemed to hold boundless opportunity. The yearning that had led so many across the Atlantic Ocean in the two hundred years since Jamestown had been founded still stirred in their descendants and pushed them westward.

One of the most popular and involved topics of that period focused on religion. The America of the age featured many god-fearing people among the populous, and the race for converts among the many churches was intense. Amid the atmosphere of truth-finding and in the free environment provided by the new republic of the United States, the table was now fully set for the restoration of the Lord's gospel. To many, the restoration of the Lord's church and authority is the greatest event of the world save for the Lord's mission on earth itself. What began in upstate New York in 1820 would change the world forever. It would also unleash every contemptible tactic the adversary could fling into the path of Joseph and his followers. And yet, as the Lord has proven time and time again, his work cannot and will not be thwarted. Over the course of the next ten years, Joseph would receive the gold plates, translate and then publish them as the Book of Mormon, begin the practice of missionary work, and organize The Church of Jesus Christ of Latter-day Saints.

Approximately a year after the Church had been organized, Joseph Smith and his family moved to Kirtland, Ohio, where he received a revelation indicating that Independence, in the relatively new state of Missouri, was to be the central place of Zion.[36] In an interesting sense of irony, the spring of 1820 saw the passage of the Missouri Compromise in the same season the Father and the Son were appearing to Joseph for the first time. Designed to calm sectional tensions over slavery, it enabled the admission of Missouri as the 24th state—a slave state, a year later.[37]

Over the course of the next seven years, members of the Church, slowly at first, began moving to western Missouri, where they encountered a local citizenry less than thrilled to have them as neighbors. By the time Joseph and his family arrived in early 1838, most of the Church's members were there, tensions with the local populace had peaked, and mob violence had forced the saints to vacate Jackson County for Liberty and Far West.[38]

Problems and persecution persisted, culminating in late October of 1838, which brought about Missouri Governor Lilburn W. Boggs' Executive Order 44, known as the extermination order, which gave state forces the authority to exterminate or drive a "Mormon" from the state.[39]

Just a few days later, a 240-man, unauthorized militia killed seventeen men and boys from the Church, drove off horses and livestock, and stole what they could grab in what came to be called the Hawn's Mill Massacre.[40]

Then, on December 1, in another blow to what seemed to be a never-ending string of adversity, Joseph and five others were incarcerated in Liberty Jail on trumped-up charges of crimes against the state.[41] After years of turmoil, the unthinkable had occurred, and the shell-shocked saints were at a loss of what to do. By the following February, with their prophet still in jail and the threat of the extermination order looming over them, the Saints began to leave Missouri for Illinois.

It was during this period—from December 1, 1838, to April 6, 1839—that some of the greatest revelations on adversity were received by the prophet Joseph Smith. Holed up in a lower-level fourteen-by-fourteen-foot cell with stone walls containing only two narrow, barred windows, a cold stone floor with only straw to sleep on, and a ceiling just over six feet high, Joseph and his cellmates endured freezing winter weather, foul odors, food that made them sick, illness, and threats and insults from hateful prison guards.[42] As days passed into weeks and weeks passed into months, the prisoners' suffering worsened as they endured great emotional, mental, and physical challenges.

Throughout the history of the world, the scriptures are replete with episodes where God tried his faithful in the furnace of affliction. This life was never meant to be easy. The fall of Adam brought a fallen state where the earth and its inhabitants became susceptible to hardship, sickness, temptation, and trial. In short, adversity entered the equation. However, that element had been planned since the beginning; part of God's plan required us to endure adversity to become like Him. The prerequisites for godhood included our ability to stay steadfast and overcome.

Our children must understand that adversity will come. Our imperfect world means different circumstances and experiences for all. While some of God's children are born into poverty or abuse, others are born into circumstances where wealth and opportunity abound. Some come into mortality without ailments while others are impaired with lifelong disabilities. Simply put, life isn't fair, and we can be impacted by events of our own making as well as events that are completely beyond our control.

The wondrous news is that the Atonement of Jesus Christ goes beyond the saving grace that enables us to become perfect and free from sin. The Savior also suffered every adversity we would encounter in life, from small disappointments to tragic occurrences. Through this, the

Atonement becomes the great equalizer; all our earthly experiences that seem so disparate will ultimately find common ground and be for our good. His time in the Garden of Gethsemane is what enables Him to provide comfort in those moments when we might feel comfortless. It is those moments of reflection that enable us to endure adversity.

In 2005 and 2006, I had no idea that a housing bubble was about to send the winds of adversity into my life. Notwithstanding, as the mortgage crisis grew and sent ripples through the market, housing prices began to fall, and thousands of homeowners walked away from their mortgages. Suddenly the value of securities backed by many of these mortgages dropped in dramatic fashion, and investment banks found themselves in serious trouble. By December of 2007 and into 2008, what came to be known as the Great Recession was in full swing, and the ensuing crisis and bailout is now part of history.

With the industry in turmoil, I found myself on the short end of a bank contraction as the market I managed was closed. Given the challenges of the economy, my efforts to consult provided meager resources, and the strain became great. As my period of unemployment turned from days to weeks and then months, the hardship of our situation and the despondency I felt seemed unbearable. As I spent countless hours pleading with the Lord for strength and asking to be delivered, I felt the loneliness and despair that comes during trials. Nonetheless, I felt His power and His love and felt the Spirit teaching me and granting me wisdom.

When I finally found work after ten long months, I asked the Lord one night why my period of adversity had lasted so long. The answer I received was gentle yet candid. Through the Spirit, I heard the Lord say, "I wasn't through with you yet." I sat silently and thought about the many times through my adversity when I'd seen the hand of God in the lives of me and my family. I recalled an evening in our home when our three-year-old daughter Eliza cried because she didn't have a robe like her sisters. Without a second of hesitation, our son Johnathan ran upstairs, grabbed one of his shirts, and cut open the front to make a robe for his little sister. While my natural mind had no desire to endure the trial again, my soul marveled at the influence of God in our lives. I realized that it was not just I who had grown through my adversity. I also came to better understand why the Lord's plan requires journeys through the refiner's fire.

It was that same fire and faith that drove the men and women of greatness who founded the United States of America. They risked everything—their lives, their families, and their property—because they saw the vision of something better for them and for all those who would come afterward. The American Revolution was fought against what seemed to be an unbeatable foe. Against all odds, they sacrificed, overcame fear, came back from defeat, and persevered to win a war they shouldn't have won. We know the outcome of that war and we often take it for granted. However, the revolution cost them dearly and lasted for seven long years.

Those early colonists would come to see that their work wasn't done. Bound together by a weak federal Articles of Confederation and stronger state governments, these early founders soon realized that a strong central government was needed.[43] Four years after the conclusion of the war, experience had taught those thirteen colonies that they were better off going at it together. Out of this debate came a new form of government and a constitution that has lasted for over two hundred and thirty years. The start of this nation was exceedingly difficult, and it was up to some of the nation's early great leaders—George Washington, John Adams, Thomas Jefferson, James Madison, Alexander Hamilton, and others—to convince the nation that each state needed to work together so America could reach its destiny. The ratification of the Constitution was never a foregone conclusion and required finesse, compromise, and the hand of God.

Within seventy years, our continued experiment in democracy was tested again when a portion of America, convinced that slavery had to stay, seceded from the union upon the election of a man who said it was time for slavery to go. Five long years later, after enduring a bloody Civil War, America again began moving forward. However, adversity has continued as our nation has struggled through two world wars where the outcomes were never certain, not to mention severe economic slumps, racial inequality, and other societal storms that have filled the pages of our history. What we see today—a free country that stands as a beacon to the world—has been built over a period of over two hundred years through adversity and conquest. We stand on the shoulders of these patriots, statesmen, prophets, pioneers, leaders, and ancestors. We are the beneficiaries of their toil and their vision, and it is incumbent upon us to stand with them and preserve the legacy they left us, much of which was built amid great adversity.

As a father, I've found it particularly challenging to watch my children go through difficulties. Our knee-jerk reactions as parents are to save them from hardship and make things easy for them. And yet, the ability to endure adversity is one of the great character traits we are here to learn. The sooner our children learn that adversity comes, the faster they'll learn how to handle it. As hard as it was for him, my father allowed me to go through those struggles, and yet I always knew he was right there with me. It was his advice and his assurances that I could persevere that enabled me to endure and grow through the process. I learned that each trial prepared me for those still to come. It falls to us to teach our children that adversity will come and that their ability to overcome will depend upon their faith, hard work, and hope in God. When we do so, we commit ourselves to Him, His work, and His promise that we can become like Him. As a friend of mine once said, we're all on an exodus to come to know God. This coming to know God is a pivotal part of our time in mortality. While adversity serves a purpose in our development, it also humbles us and helps us realize how much we rely on the Lord.

When our youngest son was born with his diaphragmatic hernia (ironically enough, this event occurred two weeks after losing my job in 2009), he was rushed to Primary Children's Hospital, leaving JoAnn and me—unsure of whether he would live—alone to await her release from the hospital the next day. As time crawled by that night, she sat in her bed without the baby she had carried for nine months. Feeling despondent and hopeless, she turned heavenward and quietly sang the prayerful words of "Abide with Me; 'Tis Eventide." At that moment, a rush of peace, love, and hope swept over her, and she knew, despite the outcome of our son's life, that all would be well. That experience gave her great appreciation for the apostles who asked the resurrected Jesus to "tarry" with them a little longer.

During our sojourn as fathers, there will be many moments when we'll feel overwhelmed, worried, and exhausted and will long for simpler days. Unfortunately, there is no escaping this very normal element of life. What we must remember is that joy and greater adventure await us just around the bend. Adversity does pass, and greater days always lie ahead.

For Joseph and his companions in Liberty Jail, the last days of March left them feeling as if they could bear no more. In this state of despair, Joseph Smith sought the Lord's intervention and received a revelation that has strengthened those under affliction for decades. After recording the many cruelties and hardships they'd endured, Joseph uttered those now-famous words recorded in Doctrine and Covenants 121:1–2:

> O God, where art thou? And where is the pavilion that covereth thy hiding place? How long shall thy hand be stayed, and thine eye, yea thy pure eye, behold from the eternal heavens the wrongs of thy people and of thy servants, and thine ear be penetrated with their cries?

Joseph's answer, an anthem to suffering saints in Missouri and thousands since, came in Doctrine and Covenants 121:7–8 and 122:7–8.

My son, peace be unto thy soul; thine adversity and thine afflictions shall be but a small moment; And then, if thou endure it well, God shall exalt thee on high; thou shalt triumph over all thy foes. . . . And if thou shouldst be cast into the pit, or into the hands of murderers, and the sentence of death passed upon thee; if thou be cast into the deep; if the billowing surge conspire against thee; if fierce winds become thine enemy; if the heavens gather blackness, and all the elements combine to hedge up the way; and above all, if the very jaws of hell shall gape open the mouth wide after thee, know thou, my son, that all these things shall give thee experience, and shall be for thy good. The Son of Man hath descended below them all. Art thou greater than he?

The Lord's promises are sure, and, amid adversity, we can indeed look to God and know He is with us.

On April 6, 1839, Joseph and his friends finally left Liberty Jail, bound to appear before a hearing in Boone County, Missouri. A few days later, while they were en route, their guards turned a blind eye and allowed Joseph and his brethren to escape.[44] God delivered them. After four-and-a-half long months in jail, their prayers were answered, and they joined their families in Illinois.

While scouting for a new home along the banks of the Mississippi, Joseph Smith arrived in the small Mississippi River town of Commerce. No doubt struck by the beauty and peacefulness of the scene, he purchased land and built a city that would ultimately house over twelve thousand people (more by some historical accounts).[45] With ownership rights in hand, Joseph selected a name for his new city that, when translated from Hebrew, meant "beautiful situation, or place."[46] Many saints would come to refer to their new home as City Beautiful. Here, under blue skies, sunshine, and canopies of oak trees humming with sounds of cicadas, Nauvoo was born. Within months the drained swamp began to give way to lush green grasses and fertile farms while red brick buildings and homes sprouted in vivid contrast. Topping it off, sitting on the hill with its sweeping view of the Mississippi, Joseph and the saints would build their house of God, a gleaming white temple.

When we first visited Nauvoo, I, like so many others, was struck with the beauty of the place. I was awed by the vivid colors of the temple, the buildings, and the fields against the backdrop of the Mississippi River and deep blue skies. Nauvoo was indeed a city beautiful.

The temple was also a vital part of the story of a people who, through great adversity, came to know God. I immediately understood why Nauvoo was so loved and why it was so hard for the early saints to leave.

In my mind, I could hear Joseph's words. His was a life of great adversity, and yet his vision of the greatest work in the world never faltered. He knew that among the noise and chaos of the world, God's work would march quietly yet majestically forward until it was completed and the Savior would come. In his epistle to the Saints he wrote, "Brethren, shall we not go on in so great a cause? Go forward and not backward. Courage, brethren; and on, on to the victory! Let your hearts rejoice, and be exceedingly glad. Let the earth break forth into singing" (Doctrine and Covenants 128:22).

— 9 —
Say Uncle
Lessons on Living

*"We stood there gawking as if Aunt Marie were
in the kitchen splitting an atom."*

In December of 1946, RKO Pictures released a motion picture that created a Christmas tradition for generations to come. Writer and director Frank Capra couldn't have imagined the cult-like following his holiday epoch *It's a Wonderful Life* would gain.[47]

A charming movie set in a fictional all-American town, *It's a Wonderful Life* tells the life story of one George Bailey, a young boy growing to adulthood with dreams of grandeur and success. Set within the waning years of World War II with flashbacks to the 1910s, 1920s, and 1930s, this beloved movie captured the excitement of an era teeming with wartime heroes, national pride, and an economy on the fringe of creating one of the greatest booms in history. It was the growing up of what famed journalist Tom Brokaw referred to as "The Greatest Generation."[48]

From his earliest recollections, George Bailey, played by the great actor Jimmy Stewart, had dreams of travel, adventure, and success. From his viewpoint, his quaint hometown of Bedford Falls could never hold him. But George's attempts to leave his home and conquer the world were delayed and thwarted by one seemingly unfortunate event after another. Despite his wonderful family and the good he did through his savings and loan, feelings of failure and disappointment were never far from his mind. The story's pivotal point occurs when, facing financial ruin, George ponders what so many others ponder during moments of despair—that perhaps the world would've been better had he never been born.

The profound element of this story is that it imitates real life in such a sensitive way. How often have we felt like George Bailey as shattered dreams, failures, and tragedies have come into our lives? It's during times such as these that our vision of God's glory, his plan, and our foreordained mission are so easily shrouded by clouds of despair. Like the fictional George Bailey, we question our value. I, like so many other fathers, have felt these emotions. In this state of disappointment, it's easy to forget about all the good we're doing. If we're trying each day to the best of our abilities, we can gain comfort in the knowledge that those are things that God asks of us and that he has promised to help us with. When the adversary tries to make us feel less than who we are, we need to stay the course and give it our best.

In this fictional story, George is given the unique opportunity to see how the years of his existence would have been had he never been born. Suddenly, he sees the importance of his life and the vast impact he had on people and events without ever realizing it. Clarence, George's assigned guardian angel, speaks to all of us when he says to George, "Strange, isn't it? Each man's life touches so many other lives that when he is not around, he leaves an awful hole . . ." That said, each of us holds an important place in the world, and our lives and efforts impact and build others in ways we can't comprehend. Regardless of age or station, our days of teaching and influence never end. We should always remain anxiously engaged in lifting others. There are grandchildren, nieces, nephews, and children in our neighborhoods, wards, and other areas of influence to whom we can give encouragement, acceptance, and love. We should never stop looking for those opportunities to use our love and abilities to influence others for good.

Like all families of that era, the world war that immediately preceded the making of *It's a Wonderful Life* dramatically impacted my extended family. As President Franklin Delano Roosevelt addressed the United States Congress on December 8, 1941, he described the preceding day as "a date which will live in infamy." His prediction has proven correct.

Just before 8:00 on the morning of December 7, 1941, over 350 fighter, bomber, and torpedo planes from the Imperial Japanese Navy launched a military strike against the United States Naval Base at Pearl Harbor, Hawaii. The surprise attacks, which came in two separate waves, sunk two U.S. battleships; destroyed 188 U.S. aircraft; damaged six other battleships, three cruisers, and three destroyers; and killed over 2,400 Americans, bringing the United States into a world war.[49] The benefit of history provides us with the knowledge of our victorious outcome. But in 1941, with Germany's power at its peak and Japan's location requiring two theaters of war, America was unnerved to say the least.

In the spring of 1943, World War II touched my dad's home for a second time when his older brother, my Uncle Bert, graduated from high school was immediately drafted, and followed my Uncle Neldon into war. Two-plus years, one shot up knee, one shot up shoulder, and two purple hearts later, Uncle Bert returned home—changed forever. He would never talk about the war and was bothered by those who glamorized it. When I later learned that he'd watched helplessly as his friend was shot and killed in a foxhole that he had just crawled out of, I knew a little more clearly why the war had had such a significant impact on his life. It was one of the experiences in the tapestry of his life that made him who he was and contributed to the impact he had on his family.

Like the fictional George Bailey, our lives, like pebbles thrown into a pond, send small ripples far beyond what we realize. The importance of every life is revealed in the way we accomplish good through each other. My life has benefitted from uncles, aunts, grandparents, and associates who wielded strong influence and offered love and wisdom at times when I needed them most. My uncles were good fathers who were also aware of the positive impact they could have on their nieces and nephews. As time has marched on, I've come to appreciate the indelible impressions my uncles made upon my life. This became especially pronounced when the first of my dad's brothers, my Uncle Bert, passed away. He, like my other uncles as they've left mortality, left a big void in my life. As I thought about each one, I've come to realize that they all had much in common. The most profound of these traits was their love of living.

It's telling that our Heavenly Father often refers to the plan of salvation as the plan of happiness. While it's true that He created the plan for our ultimate eternal happiness, He also wanted us to be happy during our earthly probation. Imagine that. The travel posters that promoted our trip to mortality weren't laced with images of tragedy and hardship. Our Heavenly Father sent us here to be happy, and happiness is a characteristic that He no doubt possesses. Gordon B. Hinckley, the fifteenth president of The Church of Jesus Christ of Latter-day Saints, stated, "In all of living have much of fun and laughter. Life is to be enjoyed, not just endured."[50]

I was always amazed at how positive President Hinckley was and how much he encouraged us to be also. While there are some who suffer from severe mental or emotional difficulties that aren't easily treated, many of us know that happiness is within our control. Many a motivator tells us that our joy isn't based upon events but how we respond to them. We've all met individuals who have remained a force for happiness and good despite having intense challenges or tragedies in their lives. However, there are many who, despite great blessings, fail to see the good in life and remain in a self-imposed exile in a state of misery. How do we avoid the pitfalls that can lead us to despair?

It's been said, "If you could envision the type of person God intended you to be, you would rise up and never be the same again."[51] What an empowering thought. When our understanding of this principle is combined with the knowledge and acceptance that we are literal sons and daughters of our Heavenly Father, we begin to see the great God-given, untapped potential and power that lie within all of us, both now and in the eternities. Our Father in Heaven sent us here to be happy and to progress, and He certainly gave us the tools to do so. A few years ago, I sat with my then eleven-year-old daughter Eliza at the kitchen table. I watched her as she stared out our bay window into a beautiful, sunny morning, with a big smile on her face. When I asked her what she was thinking about, she simply said "I am just so happy." Her smile and joy were contagious. Certainly, the journey of life is what we make of it.

Another important element of living happily is having the desire to create happiness. Too often we allow the world to tell us what will make us happy. In our zeal to give our children everything and purchase happiness, we forget that happiness comes in simple pleasures and time spent together. We can become so caught up in entertaining our children that we fail to live each day and recognize how endearing simple family traditions become to them.

When it came to tradition, nobody did it better than my dad and his three brothers. They gathered the family together for every calendar holiday from Easter through New Year's Eve. Scattered in between were vacations, Grandma's birthday, and any other excuse they could invent for getting together. They knew that this was the stuff life was made of, and they made my life so rich.

You can do the same thing. Talk with your wife and children and create traditions, both large and small. You'll find that these traditions will draw your family closer together and enable better communication.

Thanksgiving always kicked off the festive holiday season when we gathered at my grandmother's house on Salt Lake City's west side.

We packed into her simple, cozy home on 900 West, which hung heavy with the aromas of turkey, stuffing, vegetables, and pies. The house was warmed by the yellow glow of living room lamps, steamed windows, and loving uncles and aunts. When it was time for dinner, we enjoyed the veritable feast of food, seated side by side on chairs and trunks surrounding one long table on the long, crowded, enclosed back porch. Capping the day was football on television paired with the real thing played across the street on the Chapman Library lawn.

The season culminated with Christmas, which was a three-day course of celebrations. It began with the family Christmas party on Christmas Eve that got its start in the mid-1950s when Steve Allen still hosted *The Tonight Show* and the Dodgers were still in Brooklyn. Each holiday consisted of the same time-honored traditions at the same locations.

The clear mark that my dad and his brothers were anything but amateurs was exhibited by the lunch they had together every year to plan the meals for my family's annual deer hunt in October. The planning lunch was as much a tradition as were the meals we ate in my Uncle Bert's camper every year—stew, rolls, steak, fried potatoes, and creamed corn. Being raised by my dad and his three brothers was like being raised by the writing team from *Fiddler on the Roof*. Further, they showed us the joy of being involved in the planning. I've found that a good part of the excitement is in the planning of those magical details that make things so memorable.

You don't have to be a travel agent or expert organizer to create the magic. Go at your pace and use your strengths—I promise you that your children will love whatever efforts you put in.

When the first of these "four masters" passed away, I felt the irreplaceable void that occurs when any close loved one passes away. My Uncle Bert left a large impact on those he touched. Terminally happy, especially around his family, he made everyone feel important and was always proud of our accomplishments. He manned his own cheerleading section as he supported all our endeavors; his main objective was for us to know how proud he was of us and to ensure our happiness.

After he returned from the Pacific theater of World War II, Uncle Bert went to Utah State University and married his high school sweetheart, Marie. They both graduated in education and settled in Tooele, Utah, where they lived their lives as educators. Uncle Bert played and coached every sport well and ultimately became a high school administrator. Meanwhile, Aunt Marie, a junior high home economics teacher, could put out a spread of food that rivaled anything from the kitchen of Julia Child.

Of all my memories of Uncle Bert, the tradition I remember most is the Boxing Day gathering we had at his home every year on the day after Christmas. The ride to Tooele was just long enough to create great anticipation and that sense of traveling "over the river and through the woods." We all felt the zest of excitement as we piled into different cars with various cousins and began the long-awaited journey. As we rounded the bend in the highway separating the south end of the Great Salt Lake and the north end of the Oquirrh Mountain range, our cars veered west toward what looked like the edge of the lake and then south where, at long last, we'd catch our first glimpse of the Tooele Valley. The distant lights of Tooele and the snow-covered east mountains provided the perfect picturesque backdrop in the cold, December twilight. Twenty minutes later we would arrive at Uncle Bert and Aunt Marie's snow-covered house, basking in the glow of multi-colored Christmas lights on the roof, the well-lit Christmas tree visible in the corner of the front window, and steam on every windowpane—proof that Aunt Marie's kitchen was working at full power.

Uncle Bert always left the front door open so he could see us coming, and as we would bound up the sidewalk, there he was with the screen door open, his sturdy frame filling the doorway and his booming voice inviting us to "come on in!"

Once inside, uncles, aunts, and cousins packed the living room and television room to discuss the season amid the warm, soft glow of table lamps and the endless stream of nuts and M&M's that filled the candy bowls strewn all over the house. As part of the evening ritual, my cousins and I would casually saunter over to the dining room table in the small alcove to get a sneak peek at the evening's meal. Aunt Marie's kitchen prowess was at its pinnacle on the day after Christmas, and we could never resist the temptation to steal a glance at the master in her own inner sanctum. As we looked over the table, already full of everything imaginable, there stood Aunt Marie through the doorway into the kitchen. My cousins Colette and Halceyn and the other aunts worked with her, still busily cooking and sending more delicacies into the alcove. We stood there gawking as if Aunt Marie were in the kitchen splitting an atom.

The sights, sounds, smells, and emotions of Uncle Bert and Aunt Marie's house on the day after Christmas are as vivid today as they were then. They knew how to create the joy of living, and I can still see the love and happiness in their twinkling eyes. As Uncle Bert's hearty laugh filled both the house and our hearts, we knew how important we were to him. His love of life and his methodical planning of traditions changed the lives of all of us. To this day, when I think of those gatherings, my heart aches to be back there again.

One of my father's lasting memories of growing up in Castle Dale was a tradition the whole town celebrated together. During each Christmas season, the townspeople would gather in a square at the center of town and enjoy a large teepee-style bonfire. There they would visit and sing Christmas carols as the children excitedly awaited the night's crowning event. Finally, at the appointed hour, St. Nick made his grand entrance, arriving—depending upon the weather—in either a horse-drawn sleigh or a horse-drawn wagon. As the crowd welcomed him with cheers, Santa jostled to the front, where he met each child and gave them a simple brown bag with an orange, an apple, a handful of nuts, and some hardtack candy. It was a simple pleasure, a simple tradition—that always lingered and held a place in my dad's heart.

We often look nostalgically back in time at those seemingly perfect, frozen-in-time traditions and view them as a thing of the quaint past. The fact that time moves on, families grow, and communities change doesn't change the fact that Christmas still comes to Tooele and Castle Dale. People naturally search for those things that will build family and create happy memories. Through it all we discover that it's not as much the event that holds the memory as it is the people involved and the emotions created. I've found that traditions are a wonderful process of creation—always evolving and never completed. And for those who grew up in homes that lacked those traditions, remember that every tradition started with someone, somewhere.

The wonderful thing about traditions is that they can come in any manner and begin at any time. On an autumn evening, JoAnn decided to light a candle for our dinner. Throughout the meal, our three-year-old son Johnathan kept asking us if we were "having fun." The next evening, he asked her if we could bring out the "having fun candle" again. Our five-year-old son equated family fun to a simple candle, and an unplanned gesture created a family tradition. So many simple things can become traditions. Movie night, homemade pizza night, favorite TV shows, Saturday hikes in the summer, outings to see the autumn leaves, hot dogs over the backyard firepit—the possibilities are endless. Let your children help create the magic. Our efforts to create joy and a love of life for our families will establish close family relationships, a pattern of seeking happiness, and the good things in life that will last a lifetime. They remind us that there is grandeur in simplicity.

One of the great lasting legacies we can leave our families might be classified as spiritual traditions. When Naaman, the great Syrian general, heard that Elisha the prophet could heal his leprosy, he quickly traveled the distance to Elisha's home in Israel. As Naaman stood at

Elisha's door expecting a personal audience, the great Old Testament prophet sent his servant to instruct his Syrian visitor to wash himself in the Jordan River seven times. Naaman was furious. Insulted that Elisha wouldn't come out to him personally and enraged that the prophet would make such a seemingly elementary and ridiculous suggestion, Naaman stormed away. He expected a grand miracle befitting an important man.

In 2 Kings 5:13–14, Naaman's servants helped him swallow his pride. "And his servants came near, and spake unto him, and said, My father, if the prophet had bid thee do some great thing, wouldest thou not have done it? how much rather then, when he saith to thee, Wash, and be clean? Then went he down, and dipped himself seven times in Jordan, according to the saying of the man of God: and his flesh came again like unto the flesh of a little child, and he was clean."

As our families seek happiness in the face of life's trials and difficulties, we pray intently and search the words of prophets and apostles, looking for grand solutions that might help us with our challenges. And yet, like Naaman, we don't always see the great wisdom in consistently implementing those simple spiritual traditions that the prophets have promised will change our lives. Time and time again we're taught to pray and study together as a family, keep the Sabbath Day holy, spend time together, eat together, and teach one another. And yet, looking for some magical elixir to solve our plight, we look toward heaven as if to say, "Isn't there anything else?"

When our children are physically sick, we take whatever time or means necessary to make them whole. If we seek to be physically fit, we spend whatever time or means necessary to achieve it. When we have a professional, educational, or recreational goal or desire, we work at it nonstop until the goal is achieved. And yet, when it comes to being spiritually strong, we find it difficult to take the small amounts of time necessary to eat together, talk together, pray together, and study together.

Like Naaman, our focus is on the bigger things as opposed to faithfully bathing in the River Jordan.

As fathers, as patriarchs, it's our duty and our responsibility to lead out in these efforts. It may be challenging to find the time and energy to do these things; however, it's one of the most important roles we play. Gathering our families together is vital in helping our children learn how to maneuver in the world, and there are four areas where our efforts can begin—family prayer, family gospel study, family dinner time, and family fun time. We've been given the tools to be successful; all we need to do is make it a priority, set aside the time, and act. When I've found my life to be so complex that I can't see through it, I've forced myself to simplify. Often the hardest thing about achieving a goal is committing to the change that is required to accomplish it. Once we understand that the spiritual lives of our families are at stake, we will gladly sacrifice other, less important activities to help ensure our success.

When Alma gave instructions to his son Helaman, his last expression in Alma 37:47 included this statement: "Yea, see that ye look to God and live." I can think of no piece of advice that could eclipse those words: "look to God and live." Looking to God draws us closer to Him, enables us to understand His will, protects us, and reminds us of who we are and what matters. This is what enables us to truly live, both here in mortality and in the eternities.

Lessons on living can bring about so much joy and meaning to our lives. So many small moments can be easily lost in the shuffle, and once those are gone, they're gone forever. Let us make concerted efforts to create joy and happiness in family traditions as well as strength and comfort in spiritual ones, for surely the days will come in our children's lives when they will be blessed by both.

The build-up in the story of *It's a Wonderful Life* leaves the viewer truly feeling sorry for the loveable and relatable George Bailey. Just when things can't seem to get any worse, they do. And yet, the story's simple yet dramatic conclusion brings tears to my eyes and a lump to my throat every time I see it. As George Bailey's guardian angel comes to the end of his assignment, he states, "You see George, you really had a wonderful life." George's opportunity to view his life through a different lens allowed him to see the people he had influenced and the lives he had touched without ever knowing it. Most importantly, he saw how fortunate he was to have the love and devotion of his family. George's great discovery came not in adventure, wealth, or fame; it came in discovering the true happiness that comes from living.

In the movie's final scene, George, back in the present, rushes home to find his family. Upon his arrival, he's greeted with hugs, kisses, and tears by his wife and children. A team of stodgy bank examiners has come to take him to jail. However, George has come to realize that life is all about living. While the tangible things of life can be taken away, the intangibles cannot.

As George's wife pulls him into the living room in front of the family's Christmas tree, the room begins to fill with all those people who have been blessed, helped, and strengthened by George Bailey. In a matter of a few short moments, friends from near and far arrive with their own hard-earned savings to repay George for all his kindnesses and help him in his time of need. As they fill the Bailey living room to celebrate friendship and joy, George's younger brother raises a glass of Christmas cheer and toasts his older brother with the story's profound message of living and what really matters: "To my big brother George, the richest man in town!"

— 10 —

The Best Cheeseburger in the World

Lessons on Worth

"'The works' meant pickles and onions."

It was a beautiful autumn day. The leaves were changing, college football was in full swing, and I was a month into another fall semester at Brigham Young University. Among the many things I always had in common with my dad was a love for autumn. The combination of brilliant fall colors, college days, cool weather, and the approaching holiday season put a glow on everything for us. Regardless of his age, when autumn rolled around, I'd still hear my dad describe his longing to go back to a tree-lined college campus, and I came to feel that same yearning.

During this time, I was an intern with a United States congressman, and so each Friday I made the journey from classes in Provo to the Federal Building in Salt Lake City. On this particular Friday, my dad called and asked me to meet him for lunch. He'd also passed along to me his love of soda fountain counters, cafés, and hamburger spots, and he was ready to introduce me to another one. He earned his stripes in this noble endeavor while sitting at the soda fountain counter in Castle Dale's

Hunter Drug. Over the course of his life, his was a journey of culinary delight, moving like a gypsy from one delicious oasis to another. What a way to travel.

My dad started at Utah State University and then spent his last three years at the University of Utah right smack in the middle of the heyday of the 1950s. He played in the University of Utah's nationally acclaimed marching band, traveled with the football team by train, and drove a 1953 Chevy. No wonder he wanted to go back. In order to pay for college, dates, and gas for the Chevy, he worked part time as a janitor at Salt Lake City's old police station on First South and State Street. One day after work he stumbled across another hamburger jewel right across the street—a small diner named Snappy Service.

Shortly thereafter, in 1957, a young, fresh-from-the-military, twenty-two-year-old named Morris Daras was passing through town. He took what he thought was a temporary job in a temporary city as Snappy Service's newest fry cook.[52] Known to his customers as Morrie, his temporary station soon became permanent. In 1968, after Snappy Service had moved around the corner onto State Street, Morrie blessed his cheeseburger posterity when he bought the whole operation and became, along with Snappy Service, an institution. For the next forty-plus years, he served his own brand of masterpieces to the delight of breakfast and lunch crowds.

Snappy Service was no ordinary place. About forty-two feet long by fifteen feet wide with a small storeroom in the back, it seemed placed by Providence in the middle of a city block. Those who had never been graced by the Snappy Service experience said it looked out of place. I, on the other hand, thought everything around it looked out of place. Regardless, this small shoebox of a building beckoned the hungry traveler with savory aromas wafting through the propped open door in the summer and with steam on the windows in the winter. Either way, in any season, I could never pass it up.

Inside, its L-shaped counter had just fourteen stools, and if they were all occupied, you stood just a few feet behind, leaning against the south wall and waiting for a one-way ticket to cheeseburger paradise. My favorite spot was on the short side of the "L" with my back to the State Street–facing windows where I had a bird's-eye view of the grill. Standing behind the long side of the "L" with both hands at rest on the counter, Morrie stood in control of the house, waiting to look you in the eye and say, "Whad'ya have?" My order was always the same, a cheeseburger and fries, to which Morrie's reply was, "The works?" "The works" meant pickles and onions. My two-word reply was just as succinct. "No onions." Once you became a regular, Morrie registered your order in his steel-trapped mind, and before long, his simple query when I walked in the door was, "No onions?"

From there the whole show was performed right in front of us as Morrie did that voodoo that he did so well. He threw a burger on the grill, tossed a bunch of shoestring fries into the fryer, and turned back toward us to pick up the conversation. He repeated the ritual for each customer, and with Zen-like precision knew the exact moment it was time to flip the burger, add the cheese, and shovel that beauty onto the buns that were toasting facedown on the grill. He was a true master. If you wanted a soda, he pulled a bottle out of the ice-cold water cooler, slid the top into the bottle cap opener fastened to the underside of the counter, and popped the cap off before placing it right in front of you. I'd never realized that short-order cooking was an art medium until I watched Morrie.

The food wasn't the only joy to be had at Snappy Service. The conversation was always lively. Morrie typically led the dialogue, and everyone seemed to want his attention and approval. It didn't matter whether you wore a pressed business suit or a flannel shirt with a pack of Lucky Strikes in the front pocket—everyone's opinion got equal billing from Morrie. And so there we sat, side by side and shoulder to shoulder, truck drivers, lawyers, bankers, and construction workers. We all checked our egos and class differences at the door for the privilege of Morrie's burgers, chili, and meat pies. It wasn't just lunch; it was an experience. And, without ever knowing it, Morrie showed us all that each man and woman was equal, regardless of class or station. Our worth wasn't determined by what we wore, where we lived, or what we did for a living. It was determined by something deeper and less tangible that lay beneath the surface. It was fascinating to watch.

In Luke 15:4–6 in the parable of the lost sheep, The Lord said, "What man of you, having an hundred sheep, if he lose one of them, doth not leave the ninety and nine in the wilderness, and go after that which is lost, until he find it? And when he hath found it, he layeth it on his shoulders, rejoicing. And when he cometh home, he calleth together his friends and neighbours, saying unto them, Rejoice with me; for I have found my sheep which was lost." This is one story of so many where Jesus Christ pursued, recognized, and lifted the one.

One summer several years ago, I packed our family in the Suburban and headed north for a banking convention in Sun Valley, Idaho. As I drove along the winding road that hugs the mountainside south of Sun Valley one afternoon, I came upon a big-city-type traffic jam in this beautiful, quiet piece of Idaho. As I came to a stop behind the line of parked cars, I jumped outside to see what was so mesmerizing to all the other bystanders. Peering down the road, I saw two men on horses with a herd of sheep, one in the lead and the other bringing up the rear. From outside their cars, these "city folk" on vacation stood fascinated with cameras and camcorders recording this unusual parade. We all watched in awe as the shepherds made sure each sheep safely navigated the narrow space between the road and the hillside and stayed within the watchful gaze of the shepherds.

Equally interesting to me was the reaction of the crowd. Everyone stood entranced by the large flock of sheep and their shepherds. As I observed this scene, my mind quickly went to another time and another place where other crowds of people stood watching in awe as the Master Shepherd Himself carefully watched over His flock and counted each one. Some two thousand years later and eight thousand miles to the west, there we sat by the dozens, watching this real-life image of a parable we've so often heard and yet failed to completely appreciate.

In our world of imperfection, we're accustomed to playing the averages. A 90 percent score on a college exam is deemed to be wildly successful. Baseball players who hit safely three out of every ten times at bat are in great demand and are placed strategically in the prime spots of the batting order. Banks set aside a reserve for loans they expect to default. On an individual level, we learn that people are human and mistake-prone, and we're taught to look beyond the failings and weaknesses of others as well as ourselves. Our minds are so attuned to imperfection that we plan for failures among successes. Little wonder we find it difficult to get our arms around the notion of the worth of every soul when our mind of averages views 90 percent as a great success.

A wonderful element of God's plan is how individual it really is. In Moses 1:39 we read, "For behold, this is my work and my glory—to bring to pass the immortality and eternal life of man." In all our comings and goings, in all our daily responsibilities and activities, our Heavenly Father and His Son are together in one purpose: to give immortality and eternal life to each child. That one focus is Their entire mission. With that in mind, it's easier to understand how great the worth of one soul truly is. Their plan, while created for the masses, was truly created for the one.

One of my professional experiences was working for a bank headquartered in San Francisco, California. This position required that I spend periods of time there and, during those visits, I would stay at a hotel in the city's financial district one block from our offices. As I walked to the bank each morning and then back to the hotel each evening, I often noticed familiar faces among San Francisco's homeless population.

One woman seemed to stand out in my mind. Overweight and well past middle age, she attempted to navigate the few city blocks that were her world in an old wheelchair by using her feet to move her forward. Her few belongings were carefully placed in shopping bags that she tied to the chair's handles while a large piece of cardboard, folded over many times, was stored at her side.

One evening after an unusually long day of training, I left our offices after dark and, with my mind still engaged in the world of banking, headed back to my hotel. I exited our building and began walking down the street, and I noticed this same woman, directly ahead of me, crawling out of her wheelchair to lay down against the side of a building for a night's sleep. Over her head was her large piece of cardboard, completely unfolded in a lean-to position, propped up against the side of the Walgreens drug store at the corner of Montgomery and Pine Streets. I watched as she carefully spread her coat out under the cardboard on the hard sidewalk and then, after sitting upon it, wrapped the remainder of it around her to protect her from the chilly San Francisco night.

I walked along the street toward her. I suddenly felt a strong impression to stop. With it came the anxious thoughts that accompany such an approach; I became concerned about her stability and ability to understand, not to mention my selfish concerns regarding what others might think of me. These thoughts moved at such a speed that I rationalized myself right past her and around the corner of Walgreens onto Montgomery Street. By then I determined it was too late and, hoping the awkward moment had passed, kept walking.

Within seconds I realized it had not. Again, the feeling came, this time stronger than before, to go back. Still uneasy, still uncertain, I decided to circle the block to buy some time to build up some courage and figure out what to do. As I deliberated how I might help her, I came to the most logical conclusion: I would give this poor woman some money. I turned the final corner, walked gallantly to her spot, knelt, and quickly handed her a few bills of some amount while telling her that I hoped it would help. Feeling as though I'd done some noble deed, I stood upright and, without waiting for any response from her, walked again down the street.

Once again, I turned the corner onto Montgomery, and once again the same prompting returned, telling me to go back yet again. Completely stumped yet sensing some urgency based upon the frequency of the message, I began my second trip around the block. Realizing I'd allowed my fears and discomfort to guide my actions, I decided to seek the guidance of Him who was so intent on my doing something. In the next instant, the first part of the answer came. That still small voice told me that I was to tell her something.

As I rounded Sansome Street back onto Pine Street and began the last leg of my lap, I frantically sought the answer of what I should say. Then at the last moment, just a few dozen yards from her spot, I heard that same voice say, "Tell her that I love her." The message completely threw me. Tears began to well in my eyes, and the whole experience overwhelmed me. This ignored woman, known only to the world as a nuisance and a beggar, was not forgotten by God, and He wanted her to know it. In me, a very ordinary man caught up in his own world, He found a messenger, albeit a reluctant one at first.

Much humbler than before, I walked slowly to her and knelt once again. There she lay under her cardboard protection with her old, worn coat wrapped around her. Startled at my presence, she sat up and pulled her coat tighter. For the first time I really saw her. Her clothes were worn, her teeth were black, her hair was matted, and her odor was unpleasant. While she was only an audience of one, the sacred nature of the message nearly left me speechless. Still, I looked intently at her, smiled warmly, and heard my own voice say, "God wants you to know that He loves you. He wants you to know that you are His daughter and He has not forgotten you." In her silent stare I saw the pain of so many cruel words spoken to her. I don't recall if she even said anything to me. She just looked at me for a moment before smiling and lying back down under her cardboard protection. I couldn't read her thoughts, and I had no idea as to the level of her comprehension. It didn't matter; I had delivered the message that the Lord wanted delivered.

Overwhelmed by God's love, I walked the one block to my hotel at the intersection of Montgomery and California. Trying to take the experience in, I could hardly believe I'd been privileged to deliver such a message. I couldn't even count how many other similar opportunities I'd missed to be such an instrument; however, those few minutes profoundly shaped my understanding of the worth of a soul. This physically unappealing woman, seemingly lost and forgotten on the streets of San Francisco, was still being looked after by her Shepherd.

In our world of care and burden, it's easy to become caught up in our lives and challenges. So often, however, we as individuals are a key part of God's plan. His entire earthly ministry was focused on seeking out the one. Two millennia later, the pattern is the same; He seeks and blesses the one by doing most of it through us. When we listen to and act upon the promptings of the Spirit, we become instruments in His hands to lift, bless, help, and answer the prayers of those who need ministering.

The key is to act upon these promptings. In 1999, while serving as the president of Ricks College, Elder David A. Bednar stated, "To the degree that we heed these simple promptings, then our capacity to recognize and respond to the Holy Ghost is increased. To the degree that we do not heed these simple promptings, then our capacity to recognize and respond to the Holy Ghost is decreased. We are either progressing or regressing in our ability to recognize and respond to the Holy Ghost. There is no neutral ground; there is no standing still."[53] These promptings, and the personal revelation that delivers them, are at the core of discipleship and are the basis of our personal ministries. Remember the admonition from Psalm 46:10 to "be still, and know that [He is] God."

As you do this and listen, you'll receive the personal revelation for the family you have stewardship for.

In Mosiah chapter 4, King Benjamin taught what God expects of us. In verse 16 we read, "And also, ye yourselves will succor those that stand in need of your succor; ye will administer of your substance unto him that standeth in need; and ye will not suffer that the beggar putteth up his petition to you in vain, and turn him out to perish."

As I passed this "beggar" on my first pass, I followed these verses to the letter. I assumed that I was to give her money; after all, she obviously needed it, and that gesture would satisfy her need and easily and quickly fulfill my "obligation." On that clear, cool night in San Francisco, however, I learned that a financial contribution to "those that stand in need of . . . succor" is only the tip of the iceberg. Administering to others comes in so many different forms, and God knew that this woman needed His words of kindness and His expression of love far more than she needed money.

When the Lord appeared to Moses on the Mount of Transfiguration, He reminded us of the great underestimated worth of each soul. Shortly after the Lord left, a weakened Moses was immediately tested by Satan. Calling him by name, the adversary said, "Son of man, worship me" (Moses 1:12). Moses wasn't fooled. Despite his weakened condition from having been in God's presence, he still recognized the difference in approach. Moses 1:13 reads, "And it came to pass that Moses looked upon Satan and said: Who art thou? For behold, I am a son of God, in the similitude of his Only Begotten; and where is thy glory, that I should worship thee?" Moses knew glory when he saw it. Most importantly, he knew who he was—a son of God.

This test of wills against the adversary continues to this day. In our age of twenty-four-hour-a-day news cycles, social media bombardment, and make-or-break reality television, it can become extremely easy to compare ourselves to others and focus on what the world tells us we should be and what we should pursue. The adversary makes great use of these opportunities, and he exploits our feelings of inadequacies and failure to lower our self-worth, devalue all that is chaste and wholesome, and mock the God-ordained roles of men and women. In just a few short decades, our society has indeed come to "call evil good, and good evil" (Isaiah 5:20).

Many years ago as I drove through an old Salt Lake City neighborhood, I passed a home for sale that looked as though it had been pulled out of a war-torn country and dropped on a vacant lot. I smiled at the understatement that a creative realtor had placed on the sign. In big letters at the top read the short phrase, "Must See Inside." As I drove by, it occurred to me that we all at times should have signs that read "must see inside." Whether it be thoughtless words or actions or the inability to see the good and beauty inside, we all must learn the Christlike attribute of looking inside.

America's fourth president, James Madison, has been described by some as one of the most brilliant individuals in our country's existence. Prior to his two-term presidency, he was a United States congressman, a leader in the House of Representatives, and the Secretary of State. Of all his accomplishments, he is perhaps best known as the Father of the Constitution for his key role in drafting and championing its ratification as well as authoring its first ten amendments known to us as the Bill of Rights.

In his early years, Madison attended and graduated from the College of New Jersey, today known as Princeton University, where he studied Latin, Greek, science, geography, mathematics, and philosophy. He also studied law and became fluent in Hebrew.[54] The son of a Virginia plantation owner, James Madison was brilliant, successful, and well-respected. Despite these traits, James Madison never stood out in a crowd from a physical standpoint. A sickly man much of his life, he was shy and plain looking. At less than five feet, six inches tall, Madison was our smallest president.

In some of the most important years of our nation's history, James Madison's contributions were vital. As I observe politics today and the way they're covered by the media, I must wonder if a man of his physical appearance would stand a chance. We've become mesmerized by thirty-second sound bites, physical appearance, and charisma. I often wonder who is most responsible—the media who continually covers it, or the public who seems to demand the outrageous and the beautiful. Overlooked in all of this are the modern-day James Madisons.

Our Heavenly Father implores us to love each other unconditionally for who we are on the outside and the inside. Further, He wants us to see each other not for who we are but for who we can become. That eternal perspective says it all. We are sons and daughters on an earthly journey to become as He is. This knowledge gives us a better understanding of "the one." In the eyes of the Lord, there is no law of averages.

Today, the small white building where a plainspoken fry cook taught me about worth is gone, replaced by a new high-rise office building, and Morrie has faded into retirement. But to the legions who sat shoulder to shoulder on red stools at the old L-shaped counter, the steady stream of conversation, the aroma wafting through the air, and the steam on the windows created a sense of time and place never to be forgotten. The genuine, accepting man behind the counter gave us more than the best cheeseburgers in the world. Morrie showed us the worth of a soul.

II

Believe

Lessons on Work

"Congratulations, son. You just got one more rebound than a dead man."

It was February of 1980, and as per the four-year cycle of the Winter Olympic Games since their beginning in 1924, the world was again descending upon the host city. For the second time in the history of the games, beautiful Lake Placid, New York was the world's destination. Located in upstate New York in the Adirondack Mountains, the hamlet of Lake Placid—a quaint mountain village loaded with winter sport opportunities—was a perfect spot to host the thirteenth Winter Olympiad. These games brought great excitement in the United States. The nation was reeling from a series of challenges, and Americans were looking forward to showcasing its best and reminding the world of its great messages of freedom and opportunity.

Only three months prior to the games, a group of young, extremist Islamic students had stormed the American Embassy in Iran and taken more than sixty American hostages. The country stood horrified as the United States government scrambled for solutions.

One month later, the Soviet Union deployed part of its army into Afghanistan, staged a coup, killed the Afghan president, and installed a new leader. Americans condemned the invasion, and in the few weeks leading up to the games, the United Nations General Assembly demanded the withdrawal of Soviet troops in an overwhelming majority vote. All of this came at the conclusion of a decade marked by Cold War tension, energy crises, inflation, and Richard Nixon's Watergate scandal. Hosting the Olympics gave America a much-needed shot in the arm. As the opening ceremonies proceeded on February 13th, no one could predict that a miracle was in the offing from none other than the perpetual underdogs of the Winter Olympics: the United States' men's hockey team.

The Olympics of 1980 were held in an era when the United States sent only its true amateurs to compete. The practice of allowing professionals to play for America in the Olympics wouldn't be introduced for another decade. The Soviet Union, on the other hand, had arguably the best hockey team on the planet. Led by one of the best, if not the best, goaltenders in the world, Vladislav Tretiak, the Soviets had played together for years and trained in top-notch facilities.

In exhibitions leading up to the Olympics, the Soviets compiled a record of five wins, three losses, and one tie against professional teams from the National Hockey League. And in an exhibition against the NHL All-Stars the previous year, the Soviets had blasted the best professionals in North America 6 to 0. The awe and trepidation in playing the Russians were further solidified by their Olympic play—gold medals in the previous four Winter Games.

With tryouts held in July of 1979, the U.S. Olympic men's hockey team began their exhibition play only five months before February of 1980. Their play, as usual, was average, and they'd suffered a devastating 10 to 3 loss to the Soviets in New York City's Madison Square Garden only five days before the opening ceremonies in Lake Placid. American hopes were pinned to a bronze medal at best, and the only person who spoke of beating the Soviets was the one who mattered most—the United States' head coach Herb Brooks.

Olympic play began one day before the opening ceremonies on February 12th as the Americans tied a strong Swedish team 2 to 2 in their first game of the opening round. Two days later they upset heavily favored Czechoslovakia 7 to 3 and then rattled off three consecutive victories over Norway, Romania, and West Germany. Suddenly, the surprise American team took a 4–0–1 record to the medal round to face Sweden, Finland, and the undefeated Soviet Union. And so, on February 22nd, the nation held its collective breath as the Americans faced the Soviets in the first game of the medal round.

Tensions and hopes were high in the sold-out Olympic field house, and yet the thought of this team of young amateurs defeating the mighty Soviets seemed impossible to comprehend. Olympic sports anchor Jim McKay later stated that the matchup was comparable to an All-Star team of Canadian college boys beating the 1980 Super Bowl Champions, the Pittsburgh Steelers.[55]

The Soviets struck first with a goal in the first period; however, the Americans countered when left-winger Buzz Schneider scored on a slap shot from just inside the blue line at 14:03 of the first period to tie the score. A few minutes later the Soviets scored again, and as the clock wound down, it appeared the Russians would take the lead going into the locker room. With seconds left in the first period, USA defenseman Dave Christian's slap shot bounced off Tretiak's leg pads and bounced in front of him. Splitting between two Soviets, American center Mark Johnson grabbed the lucky bounce and shot the rebound into the net past the diving Tretiak. With just one second remaining in the first period, the score was tied, and the Soviets' head coach pulled the mighty Tretiak and replaced him with backup goaltender Vladimir Myshkin.

The crowd nervously watched the second period transpire with only one goal by the Soviets, which set up a third period for the ages. Mark Johnson scored his second goal of the game when he grabbed a loose puck and tied the score about eight minutes into the third period. Just a few minutes later, USA's team captain, right-winger Mike Eruzione, stepped onto the ice for a line shift change. As he hustled to the offensive zone, USA center Mark Pavelich hit him with a pass that Eruzione shot high into the net past Myshkin, who was screened by one of his own defensemen. As the crowd erupted, Eruzione ran on the tips of his skates around the corner of the dashers and was mobbed by his teammates. With ten minutes left, the Americans had a 4 to 3 lead, their first lead of the game.

Trailing for the first time, the Soviets aggressively attacked the Americans' defensive zone. As the USA continued its unrelenting offensive attack, the Soviets seemed to panic.[56] In the final minute, the Soviets pushed the puck back into the American zone. After a couple of shots and a scramble for a loose puck, the Americans stayed strong and attempted to clear the puck out of their own zone.

With the crowd beginning to count down, sportscaster Al Michaels began his last ten seconds of the broadcast that would give him a place in history and emblazon his words in the hearts of Americans. Michaels excitedly yelled, "Eleven seconds, you've got ten seconds, the countdown going on right now! Morrow up to Silk, five seconds left in the game. Do you believe in miracles?! YES!"[57] Michaels and color commentator Ken Dryden sat in silence as the crowd went into a frenzy. The American players jumped from the bench and stormed the ice, running and jumping on the tips of their skates, mobbing each other near the United States' net in a scene I'll never forget.

Meanwhile, at center ice, the stunned Soviet hockey team stood, leaning on their sticks, watching in disbelief as this young group of amateurs celebrated the impossible. The looks on the Soviets' faces seemed to echo what so much of the world was thinking, as well as the sentiments of color commentator Ken Dryden. As the clock hit zero and Michaels screamed "YES!" Dryden, seemingly unable to conceal his thoughts, quietly uttered the word "unbelievable."

In my own living room, I cheered, I jumped, and I cried as I witnessed the incredible conclusion of this miracle of miracles. Hope had returned. We were champions, and like so often in our storied past, America had accomplished the impossible. Once again, we were bigger than life. Better yet, we'd done it at the hands of the Soviets, who always brought their best to try and prove to the world that their way was better. Two days later in a game that almost seemed anti-climactic, the Americans would beat Finland 4 to 2 to win the gold medal. To this day I can't watch those last seconds nor listen to Al Michaels calling those last eleven seconds without getting a lump in my throat and tears in my eyes. It was one of the most remarkable moments in sports I've ever seen. Watch or read *Miracle* and other stories like it with your children. They're great motivators.

When the Americans received their gold medals, the U.S. and the world caught a glimpse into this remarkable team for the ages when team captain Mike Eruzione, standing on the gold medal platform, motioned his nineteen teammates to join him. Together to the end with arms around each other, they held up the symbolic "number one" finger and celebrated on a small gold medal platform. In that "Miracle on Ice," as in so many stories of great achievement, we learn a valuable lesson that we must pass along to our sons and daughters—that they can accomplish all they desire provided they believe and are willing to pay the price.

Those ten days in 1980 were a magical time. The country came together, and new hockey fans were converted by the thousands. However, what we saw was the end result of months of dedication and hard work. This is an important lesson in considering what it takes to see the results of our work. Achievement in any realm doesn't come right away. Effort, dedication, and hard work are required. The same can be said of our most important role as fathers. Remember that we may not see the results of our hard work for many years, so be patient with your children and be patient with yourself.

Muhammad Ali, considered by many to be among the greatest heavyweights that boxing has ever seen, amassed an incredible record of fifty-six wins and five losses. His unusual style was to use his incredible speed and reflexes while remaining constantly in motion. This led to his famous quote "Float like a butterfly and sting like a bee,"[58] and his opponents were baffled. When emphasizing his success, Ali taught the value of work when he stated, "The fight is won or lost far away from the witnesses—behind the lines, in the gym, and out there on the road, long before I dance under those lights."[59]

The sporting world is ripe with messages that teach us that talent alone is never enough. When the New Orleans Jazz relocated to Salt Lake City in 1979, one of their first and best moves was to hire a comedic, basketball-savvy Brooklyn native named Frank Layden as their general manager. In the early, pre–Karl Malone and John Stockton days, wins were scarce and attendance was low. But one of the things that kept basketball fans intrigued was the humor of Frank Layden. He used to joke that when people would call to find out what time the game started, his response was, "What time can you be here?" In a game when the Jazz was getting trounced by the Boston Celtics in the glory days of the great Larry Bird, Layden was overheard in a timeout telling his players, "Forget about Boston; let's beat Bird!"

Of all Layden's quotes, the one that stands out occurred after Layden had also assumed the role of head coach. One of his famous missives was "You can't teach height," and so the Jazz was always looking to add big centers. Unfortunately, some of them came with raw talent but a questionable work ethic. After one painful loss in which his seven-foot center pulled down just one rebound, Layden approached him postgame and said, "Congratulations, son. You just got one more rebound than a dead man."[60]

Herb Brooks, the head coach of that 1980 USA hockey team, had seven short months to build a winning team. He put his team together and began a grueling process of practices and sixty-one exhibition games against teams in the United States and Europe. After an embarrassing exhibition loss to Norway, Brooks kept his players on the ice for hours in a half-lit arena, skating them back and forth between the goal line and the blue line until many of them were vomiting from the physical stress.[61] Throughout the session, he peppered them with the same question: Who do you play for? Brooks finally let them go when one of them figured it out. He didn't want them to state which college they played for; he wanted them to understand that they now played, as one team, for the USA. Brooks knew they needed to understand that the best chance they had for success was work and dedication to each other. They needed to know who they were. Those moments of fame and glory and that miraculous victory on February 22, 1980, came at a cost of failure, sacrifice, determination, and gut-wrenching work.

The success of America has come precisely the same way. Andrew Carnegie, one of the great industrialists of America, came to this country with his family from Scotland in 1848. With the Irish Potato Famine experiencing some of its worst years, the Carnegies were among close to two hundred thousand people who arrived in the United States and Canada from Liverpool's port in 1848. Along with his parents and younger brother, Andrew settled in what was then called Allegheny City, Pennsylvania, located across the Allegheny River from downtown Pittsburgh. Within just a few months, thirteen-year-old Andrew began his ascent working as a bobbin boy in a cotton factory making $1.25 a week. Working twelve-hour days that began at 5:00 each morning, he ran back and forth along the factory floor providing spinners with new bobbins and taking their used ones.[62]

Shortly thereafter, the owner of a bobbin manufacturer recognized Andrew's work ethic and offered him $2.00 a week to fire the boiler that turned the shop's nine lathes. When he was given the opportunity to be the shop's part-time bookkeeper, he still had to spend the rest of his time "bathing every newly turned bobbin in vats of crude Pennsylvania petroleum."[63]

Andrew Carnegie's life paralleled the rise of American industrialism, and he seemed placed at most every pivotal intersection of America's economic march into the future. Before turning fourteen, he became a young telegraph messenger right at the time when telegraph lines were beginning to connect major U.S. cities. By the time he was eighteen, he'd secured employment with the Pennsylvania Railroad Company. Over the course of the next forty-plus years, Andrew Carnegie would capitalize on oil that was ever increasing in demand, the growing needs and opportunities in a burgeoning railroad industry that had begun to crisscross America, and the steel business that provided products for the railroads, bridges, and sleeping cars that Carnegie built. He continued to work and, in the process, created an empire of businesses and philanthropic endeavors that left a large imprint on the American economy. In 1901, the sixty-six-year-old Carnegie sold his businesses, retired, and kept his long-standing promise to give away his fortune. Over his remaining years, Carnegie would fund close to three thousand libraries as well as provide financial gifts to entities such as universities, museums, concert halls, and hospitals.

Andrew Carnegie understood what too many people today do not; the end result can't be given freely or equally. When hearing about the famous Carnegie name, most only see the result of his life's work. And while many biographers have debated the ethics of the style of business that was prevalent in the late 1800s, Andrew Carnegie's life can be easily described by the hard work and determination that was his journey. His start as a member of a lower-income immigrant family never deterred him. Our imperfect world can never distribute equality by providing a free ride. What the world does offer to all is the opportunity to achieve that result, and it comes through hard work, sacrifice, and making our own way. When Carnegie described his work dipping bobbins in crude oil, he later said, "I never succeeded in overcoming the nausea produced by the smell of oil."[64] In those early days of exhausting, demeaning work, Andrew Carnegie came to know who he was and what he was capable of. That work became part of what defined Andrew Carnegie and instilled in him a desire for success as well as a desire to do good with it. His was a passion that fit President Theodore Roosevelt's description for hard work. Said Roosevelt, "Far and away the best prize that life offers is the chance to work hard at work worth doing."[65]

History is a sound teacher, and it's interesting to follow the path of America's success and growth from a new provincial country, struggling to find its identity, to arguably the greatest nation the world has ever seen. Colonial America was a largely agrarian society with a western boundary made up of the Appalachian Mountain range that ran from Georgia to New York and New England. In the years following the revolution, early Americans had their eyes toward new horizons west of the Appalachians. Exploration, opportunities, and innovation gathered steam, and soon the new country began to ride a new wave of prosperity focused on industrialization. This new commerce offered new opportunities, and soon the nineteenth century gave way to an industrial revolution that added even more fuel to the American economy. By the early 1900s, America had arrived as a global political, military, and economic power. That wave continued throughout the twentieth century as technological innovation moved to the forefront. While each generation has had different challenges in different eras, the core drivers of our rise to greatness have never varied from one generation to another. Hard work, determination, vision, and the freedom to pursue dreams have defined each era.

Jolene Brown, a professional speaker, author, and family business consultant from West Branch, Iowa, delivered an address at a conference where she spoke about emerging economies around the world and the drive behind its young people who are willing to work hard at any type of work to succeed. As she spoke, I was reminded of the same drive possessed by so many generations as the United States rose to prominence and prosperity. In discussing our responsibilities as parents, Jolene stated, "We owe our children the opportunity for education. I didn't say that it had to be paid for. We send them to college, and we pay for their tuition, their car, their room and board, their cell phone, and their computer, and then when they graduate, we expect them to go out and work. My question is, when did they learn to work? We must teach them about work, accountability, and responsibility."[66]

Give your children chores at an early age and work with them to accomplish both small and large tasks. Provide them with opportunities to work and hold them accountable by making sure they've completed their tasks completely. Let them earn an allowance and teach them the value of money by saving and avoiding debt.

What a great lesson for fathers and mothers. While other countries pour resources into education, we debate about whether a city is going to build a new football stadium to keep the franchise from leaving town. We're a great nation; however, our greatness was built over a long period of time. Over four hundred years have passed since Jamestown was first established. At that moment, an idea was born. It was an idea of pioneering, innovation, independence, and opportunity.

Now it falls to us. We are a bright, caring people who still fiercely believe in the idea of liberty and independence. We must make sure that affluence and power don't lead to arrogance and laziness. We've become a society that does what it wants when it wants with a tendency to let others mow our lawns and do whatever else we think we don't have time for. Further, we focus too much on the things that entertain us and give too much attention to those who provide it as opposed to focusing on what builds character.

Without a solid work ethic, our children will struggle in every avenue of their lives—education, service, careers, marriage, and parenting.

Our society is so focused on ease that advertisements bombard us with the chance to trade away our work and pay someone else to do it—all in the name of creating more leisure time. Finding leisure time is not a challenge; getting children to understand the value of work is. Additionally, there is a "get rich quick scheme" around every corner. Our children must know what the word *scheme* means and that there is no other path to success than hard work. Shielding them from this understanding robs them of the opportunity to learn how to work, build character, and find pride in, as Theodore Roosevelt said, "the chance to work hard at work worth doing."

Work also enriches lives through the many values that come with it. In the mid-1800s, a young man from America's Midwest faced failure after failure in his quest for success. When he joined the military, he left as a captain and returned as a private. He failed as a businessman and worked tirelessly to succeed at the law. During a period when it appeared he had suffered his second failed attempt to become engaged, he wrote to his friend and former law partner, "I am now the most miserable man living. If what I feel were equally distributed to the whole human family, there would not be one cheerful face on the earth."[67] He later turned to politics, where he was defeated in his first run for the state legislature and was defeated as a potential nominee to congress. He then lost in his attempts to be commissioner of the General Land Office, a state senator in 1854, a candidate for the vice presidency in 1856, and a U.S. senator in 1858. Two years later, in 1860, he finally achieved success. Abraham Lincoln was elected the sixteenth president of the United States.

Failure is a common thread of those who have achieved great heights. Basketball legend Michael Jordan said, "I've missed more than nine thousand shots in my career. I've lost almost three hundred games. Twenty-six times I've been trusted to take the game-winning shot . . . and missed. I've failed over and over and over again in my life. That is why I succeed."[68] If we use failure correctly, if we learn from it and then put it behind us, it can build great character. This process can only benefit us as it forces us to reevaluate, learn, and dig deep within ourselves to find the will to try again.

Work's companion is ambition. There's no reason why we should ever accept mediocrity in our children. While we should never let our children feel they have to be perfect, we should teach them to rise above mediocrity and seek excellence. Settling for mediocrity robs them of the vast opportunities that exist and the great God-given potential they have within them. We have no comprehension of the good that can be done with our God-given gifts when working under His direction. Further, work motivates us to set goals, strive for excellence, and shoot for the stars. Our lives need not be a series of random events that we respond and react to. We can set a course for our lives and work in a planned way to be proactive and enable our goals to become reality. Our children will be happiest at their work when they do something they love.

Next, work teaches the important traits of accountability and responsibility. Noted philosopher, theologian, physician, and Nobel Peace Prize recipient Albert Schweitzer once said that "man must cease attributing his problems to his environment and learn again to exercise his will—his personal responsibility."[69] If we are to be the authors of our successes, we must also learn to own our failings. Without the acceptance of accountability, our children will flounder and always look for places to lay blame. Lou Holtz, the legendary football coach who led the Notre Dame Fighting Irish to a 12-0 record and the 1988 National Championship, said, "The man who complains about the way the ball bounces is likely the one who dropped it."[70]

The world is full of examples of people who overcame great odds, fought for success, and worked hard to achieve their goals. As we share these experiences with our children, they'll come to appreciate that all they achieve will come at a price. Too many in our country have an attitude of entitlement. The same opportunity that was available to a poor

Scottish immigrant named Andrew Carnegie is available to us all. But it's not the end result we're entitled to; it's the opportunity to pursue it. Whether it is freedom, opportunity, heritage, comfort, education, or a career—each comes with a price. While some are paid by us, others have been paid by those who went before. Our children must understand the responsibility of pursuing things worth pursuing. They must also understand that accepting failure is not defeat. It is the determination to rise above that failure that builds character.

Nine years before his death, Theodore Roosevelt delivered a speech that included a quote that came to be known as "The Man in the Arena." Roosevelt was a man who had known both victory and defeat. He overcame severe asthma and other health ailments in his youth through vigorous exercise. Two days after the birth of his first child, his wife died of kidney failure. Eleven hours later his mother died in the same house. Despite his challenges, he went on to accomplish great feats through continuous work and determination. He built a ranch in the Dakota Territory, served in the New York legislature, and then served as the New York police commissioner all before the age of thirty. By the time he became president of the United States at age forty-two, he had served as a U.S. civil service commissioner, assistant secretary of the Navy, governor of New York, and vice president of the United States, not to mention his hero status as a colonel in the United States Volunteer Army who led the "Rough Riders" up Cuba's Kettle and San Juan Hills in the Spanish-American War. Roosevelt represented everything good about hard work and a strenuous lifestyle. His was a life of dedication to principles and an unrelenting desire to do what was right and to keep going until the work was done.

In 1910 Roosevelt said,

> It is not the critic who counts; not the man who points out how the strong man stumbles, or where the doer of deeds could have

done them better. The credit belongs to the man who is actually in the arena, whose face is marred by dust and sweat and blood; who strives valiantly; who errs, who comes short again and again, because there is no effort without error and shortcoming; but who does actually strive to do the deeds; who knows great enthusiasms, the great devotions; who spends himself in a worthy cause; who at the best knows in the end the triumph of high achievement, and who at the worst, if he fails, at least fails while daring greatly, so that his place shall never be with those cold and timid souls who neither know victory nor defeat.[71]

Remember that your children will fail. Those are the great teaching moments. Give them examples from this book of people who have failed before succeeding. And the best things you can provide are love and encouragement. Remind them that, as they work hard, their day will come.

In the winter of 2002, twenty-two years after the thrill of the 1980 Olympics, the Winter Games came to America once again. Five months prior to the Olympics' opening ceremonies in Salt Lake City, terrorists hijacked four American commercial airliners and flew them into the World Trade Towers in New York City, the Pentagon, and a field in Pennsylvania in one of the most horrific events played out on American soil. Dazed and disconsolate, Americans were endeavoring to adjust to an ever-changing world while keeping a ray of hope alive. Inside Salt Lake's Olympic stadium, the last runner with the Olympic torch entered on cue to officially open the 2002 Winter Games. The crowd erupted when the face of the runner popped up on the big screen. It was none other than the USA's hockey team captain from 1980, Mike Eruzione. To deafening cheers, Eruzione ran along the stadium track with the torch and then, joined by many of his former teammates at the base of the cauldron, raced with them up the stairs where they all put a hand on the torch and lit the Olympic cauldron. The boys of the 1980 "Miracle on Ice" had returned to the stage to reinforce to the world America's resiliency—and to bring us hope once again. Further, they brought us memories of one of the great miracles wrought from the hard work and determination of twenty young men.

12

My Very Own Greek Wedding

Lessons on Contribution

"We have not men fit for the times."

I married a cute little Greek girl. What is it about Greeks? The culture, the architecture, the food, the music, the mythology—there's just something mystical and romantic about them. At least there was with this one. The first time I saw her big blue eyes, beautiful smile, and perfect olive skin, I needed oxygen. My whole life's purpose became a plot to con her into marrying me. As my good fortune would have it, it worked.

Covering the approximate period of 800 BC to 150 BC, Greece ascended as one of the ancient world's superpowers. Proud, industrious, and passionate, the Greek people endowed the world with philosophers, artists, writers, and shipbuilders, not to mention a litany of "firsts" for centuries. During this period, Greece's maritime strength spurred colonization, and the island of Crete was of great interest to the Greeks and the world.

Located on the eastern edge of the Mediterranean, Crete sits about one hundred miles south of Greece's mainland. Bounced around between the Arab, Byzantine, Roman, Venetian, and Ottoman empires, this 160-mile-long island has been a prized strategic possession through the ages. Today, Greece's Crete is a Mediterranean masterpiece with azure skies and tranquil white beaches that match the colors that adorn my wife's Greek flag, which happens to be big enough to cover our entire garage door.

Nestled along its shores and harbors are villages lined with street cafés where wooden tables with checkered tablecloths sit invitingly under vine-covered trellises. In these cafés, Crete's famous cuisine is served up to the max. These masters of fine dining use every ounce of the herbs that grow naturally on the island and take advantage of the fruits and vegetables that flourish in Crete's long growing season. Come nightfall, entire villages light up and reflect in harbors like strands of jewels.

October 6, 1890, was a day like any other on the northern shore of Crete's western end as fishing boats bobbed up and down in the waters, trolling the Mediterranean in search of the daily catch. Meanwhile, in the small village of Vamos, five miles to the south, farmers and villagers traversed narrow hilly streets surrounded by fields of chestnut, cypress, and olive trees complimented by radiantly colored wildflowers. It was on this day in Vamos that the world quietly welcomed my wife's paternal grandfather, Dimitrios Giannikaki. What a great name.

Despite the beauties of Crete, life for Dimitrios and his four brothers and three sisters was extremely difficult. Poverty was common, and Dimitrios lost four siblings to death—one as an infant, two to starvation, and another in military service. War was common in that era, or the continual threat of it. After Greece gained its independence in 1821, Crete became a hot spot as Christian Cretans revolted against Ottoman rule. After decades of hostilities, the Ottoman Empire declared war on Greece in 1897 only to have the major European powers launch a multi-national naval force to blockade and occupy Crete after deciding the Ottomans couldn't hold it. After an autonomous state was established, Ottoman troops were sent off the island, and Crete would soon become part of Greece. In this age of uncertainty, recruitment into Greece's military was mandatory, and so amid the great hardships of their lives, Dimitrios and his brother Minoli took the limited money they had and boarded a ship for America in 1910. They left the seemingly endless hardships of the old world with the hope of finding opportunity, work, and a better quality of life—in short, the American Dream.

Ocean voyages for poor immigrants were far from the glamorous ocean crossings of today. Arriving early at the docks, Dimitrios and Minoli first had to endure the mandated physical examination by the shipping company as well as a twenty-nine-question survey before they could board.

After waiting for hours and with their exams completed and recorded, they were led like sheep with other third-class ticket holders to the ship's steerage compartment. Unable to afford first- or second-class passage, the brothers Giannikaki presented their "steerage" tickets and were led down a long concourse to a large open area where they were assigned metal berths with a thin mattress to sleep on. Located in the same section of the ship that housed the ship's cargo, controls, and engines, the conditions were crowded, dark, and unsanitary. Adding to this burdensome setting was intense crowding, limited eating areas, poor food, and inadequate bathrooms and ventilation that made for a strong stench. The only reprieve they had to break up the monotony were games of cards or chess or favorable weather days when they could go up on deck and enjoy the ocean air. However, being third-class passengers, Dimitrios, Minoli, and the countless others from steerage were given the deck space on the ship where the motion was the most turbulent and where the smell of the smokestacks directly above created a unique smell with the odors from below. These conditions, along with rough days at sea, made the journey long and arduous.

By the time they finally reached New York Harbor, many of the third-class immigrants were in a state of physical and emotional exhaustion. Thinking they had arrived and would be disembarking any minute, many passengers were surprised to find they'd arrived at the quarantine area in New York Harbor's lower bay between Staten Island and Brooklyn for another round of medical exams. Hours later, jittered and tense, the passengers again heard the stacks and felt the motion of the ship as they began to move, this time north into the harbor's Upper Bay toward Manhattan. It was here where hundreds of immigrants were overwhelmed by their first glimpse of Manhattan and the Statue of Liberty. Within a short time, the ship docked at the southern tip of Manhattan near Battery Park where the privileged first- and second-class passengers disembarked into freedom, completely oblivious to the nerve-wracked steerage class who were crossing the pier to another dock, where they were packed onto barges that took them back southwest across the harbor to Ellis Island.

As the barge carrying them docked, Dimitrios and Minoli became two of the twelve million immigrants who would ultimately pass through Ellis Island. Immediately greeted with the shouts of multiple languages, they were herded with the masses through the main doors and up to the Registry Room via a steep stairway so they could, one by one, complete the immigration screening process. Reaching the top of the stairs, the brothers met eye to eye with doctors who scrutinized their every move, searching for signs of sickness or mental conditions. As the two passed by without being stopped, they saw people in front of them and behind them walk on with a large, chalked letter on their back, signifying what ailment was suspected. Some were even forced to be disinfected and bathed before moving on.

Their next stop was the official registry desk, where they waited in turn to register and present their papers before being moved quickly to a line where they awaited a test from an eye doctor and a final legal inspection, through an interpreter, where they were asked the same twenty-nine questions they'd been asked before their passage had begun. Unknown to the Giannikakis, failure to provide the same answers they provided prior to leaving Greece would have resulted in deportation.[72] They also had to prove the ability to earn a living as well as present the results of healthy physical exams. The inability to provide either also resulted in deportation. After four or so long hours at Ellis Island, with their names changed to the English translations of their first names and the inspector's best guess at their last name, Jim and Mike Johnatakis exited the doors under the skies of the New York Harbor and the United States of America.

With all their money spent on their ocean journey, Jim and Mike found low-rent lodgings in New York City and shoveled snow all throughout the ensuing winter to buy train tickets to the coalfields of Utah. Their research had told them that many of their countrymen were there and that mining jobs were plentiful in central Utah. In the following spring, Jim Johnatakis traveled west with his brother, found work, married, and over the course of the next twenty years had a batch of eight Greek children, six of whom would live to adulthood.

Had Jim's visions of America included immediate ease and success, he would have been far afield. Coal mining consisted of ten-to-twelve-hour days in dark mines that came in two forms—dry and wet. Neither option really held an advantage over the other. While dry mining brought continuous dust, the wet version left miners in water up to their knees with the realization that wet socks were impossible to work in. It also meant an hour at home after work using a razor to cut the calluses that had formed on their feet from wet boots. Either way, the work was backbreaking, and the pay was low as miners were paid by the pound, not the hour. As if that weren't challenging enough, the process for mining coal required digging through foot after foot of rock before hitting a coal vein, and miners were paid only for coal, not for the rock they had to dig through to get to it.

Despite the difficulty of his life, Jim found joy and satisfaction in America. Jim was not only hardworking but also intelligent and enterprising. Working in a wet mine, he knew that water was pumped out of the mine daily. This resourceful Greek was always thinking. In the dry landscape of central Utah, he planted a garden on an acre of his land in the only place where there was a vast amount of accessible water—downstream from where the water was pumped from the mine. After a day of exhaustion working in the mine, he went to work running the only farm for miles around and raised chickens, rabbits, and vegetables. He then sold eggs, corn, and other produce to the miners to support his growing family. Grandpa Jim lived and worked the rest of his life in the small coal towns of central Utah for the sole purpose of giving his family something better.

The story of Dimitrios Giannikaki (Grandpa Jim) shaped the lives of his children and grandchildren in a way that nothing else could. Their appreciation and adoration of him grow with each passing Greek Easter and as the stories of his life pass from generation to generation. Each one of us can relate to Grandpa Jim, for our greatest desires are to give our family something better. Our work, our efforts, our thoughts, and our goals are all tied to building our families. Jim's fifth child, a son named Johnnie, would one day become my father-in-law. Broadly built with Mediterranean olive skin and well-defined Greek features, I first knew him as the imposing voice behind the sliding door into my new girlfriend's dining room.

On the night I arrived to pick up JoAnn for our first date, I felt as though I were listening to the *Wizard of Oz* as he announced, "Don't be late, Sis" behind the closing sliding door. At that point I considered getting her back home before we even left.

However, I quickly came to love and appreciate this man. Later in his life he joined the Church of Jesus Christ of Latter-day Saints only to have his wife pass away fourteen months later. Left to raise his five children without her, he set out to do what his father had done: he kept going and worked hard for the sole purpose of giving his family something better. Although he never had the opportunity for education beyond high school, he became a highly intelligent man with a gift for anything mechanical. He was also a masterful manager and taught himself whatever he didn't know. The two things I've come to notice and appreciate most are his mind and his hands, both of which are constantly at work.

And so began my relationship with this classic Greek family. Determined and passionate, they came complete with endless olive oil, epic stories, a lamb on the spit, strong opinions, and food that kept coming.

At my first Greek Easter, my wife's aunts converged on me with hugs and food as if I were some long-lost cousin just in from Athens. That event began what has become my continued enjoyable journey of learning the Greek root of everything and watching my father-in-law and his sisters try to out-haggle each other. Their shrewd deal-making abilities became more apparent on a November "Black Friday" when I overheard a conversation between my wife and her high-charged sister over our kitchen speakerphone. I wasn't sure if I was listening to my sister-in-law oversee her family's takeover of Walmart or Eisenhower's forces taking a beachhead on D-Day. When it comes to arguing for sport, their prowess is equally spectacular. Each one claims victory, but to the non-Greek, it's difficult to ascertain who the victor is. They are masters of their skill, and they handle it-must-have-come-from-Greece conversations in the same efficient manner that the Greeks built the Parthenon.

On a hutch in our living room sits a framed copy of an old photograph of JoAnn's young Grandpa Jim with his brother Minoli that was taken in New York City in 1910. Shortly after these two young brothers arrived in New York, each donned their only suit to record this great moment for their posterity. Proud and erect, they stood side by side with looks of great hope in their eyes. Like so many before and so many since, they had come to America to conquer their dreams.

That photograph bears only one resemblance to the ones I saw of Jim near the end of his life. Tired and old, he still held a smile and a glint of hope in his eyes. But that hope was now in the grandchildren he was holding. I never met Dimitrios Giannikaki, but I would guess that he never fully realized the dreams he had on that day over one hundred years ago when he was photographed in a New York City studio. However, through his hard work, determination, and sacrifice, his posterity would realize them. When JoAnn graduated from college and had a good position with a large banking company, I saw that pride in her father's eyes and knew that somewhere, Grandpa Jim was beaming, perfectly happy that he had made that hard voyage to America. When those lessons are remembered, the lives of each generation are blessed, and they're given greater opportunities.

You and I share common concerns and dreams. We hope that our children won't forget, and we endeavor each day to ensure their remembrance of the many sacrifices made for them. We are the benefactors and temporary possessors of a great heritage—benefactors because it has been passed to us and temporary possessors because it is our responsibility to pass it to the next generation. If my wife and I don't teach our children about Grandpa Jim and all that he did to achieve a better life, how will they learn about him? How will they come to appreciate what he did, what he worked for, and what he sacrificed for them? Most importantly, how will they learn that they have an obligation to contribute themselves?

Throughout these chapters, I've written about many of my ancestors and the difficulties they faced. The idea of immigrating to another country with nothing but a few belongings or leaving school at fourteen is both awe inspiring and hard to comprehend. Each of us has a rich past of similar stories and beginnings. Find them and share them with your children so they can better appreciate the sacrifices of their ancestry and their devotion to their posterity.

The wonder of contribution is that it can come in both big and small portions, and one successful businessman found a way to accomplish both. When Menlo Smith returned home from a mission for The Church of Jesus Christ of Latter-day Saints in the Philippines, the *Deseret News* reported that he "came home vowing to do something about the poverty he had seen."[73] With a vision for a microfinance organization in mind, Smith, along with other businessmen, founded Mentors International in 1990, whose mission would be to provide micro-loans, training, and expertise to underprivileged recipients wanting to start businesses and rise above their level of poverty.

Ten-plus years later, Mentors received an application from a man in the Philippines named Mike Espinilla. Wheelchair bound because of polio, his poverty-stricken family lived in a cement home with no flooring and simple curtains covering glassless windows. His opportunities were extremely limited, and he'd already lost his young son to a death brought on by malnutrition. However, Mike Espinilla had a gift for creating art. With an idea in his mind and having heard about Mentors International, he applied and received business training and a small $100 loan. This small amount of money would become transformational. With the loan in hand, he purchased tools and began collecting discarded fluorescent lighting tubes from the local landfill. Once he'd obtained them, he would wash out the tubes and then, putting his glassblowing skills to work, create glass figurines such as swans, flowers, and hearts for local markets. Soon orders were coming in from farther away and he had more orders than he could produce. Through the contribution of others who had the desire to lift those who needed a lift, this disabled, impoverished Filipino was given the opportunity to provide for his family, become a successful, independent entrepreneur, and see the vision of his own potential.[74] This small contribution led to one significant enough to give this man the opportunity, as the *Deseret News* reported, "to help pull himself out of poverty and to help his children do so permanently."[75]

In my home sits a small, glass-blown swan made by none other than Mike Espinilla, where it stands as a constant reminder to my family and to me of the potential we can rise to as well as the resources and opportunities we have available at our disposal. It stands as a reminder to me that there is so much more to do with our time than surf the internet, watch over one hundred channels of television, and play endless video and computer games. There is great good to be done. Find your inner decorator and identify quotes, old family photos, and other meaningful reminders that can be placed around your home for your children to see each day.

In the fictional movie *The Emperor's Club*, a history teacher at a prestigious private school for boys opens each year with a discussion about contribution. As he teaches them about a ruthless conqueror who has been forgotten in the annals of history, he offers the reasoning for the historical slight by stating, "Great conquest, without great contribution, is without significance." Then, in a reflective moment, he looks at his students and asks, "What will your contribution be?"[76] While the story is fictional, the question has deep meaning to all of us. Our families, neighborhoods, institutions, nation, and world are only as good as the contributions that our children will make to them.

Spend some time with your children and help them outline some ways that they can make a positive contribution to the world. Teach them as they set goals to always have those thoughts in mind. Lastly, help them see their strengths and then consider how they can use those to benefit their family, their community, and their world.

We must remember that what we have was bought with a price and must be preserved with a price. The America of today is vastly different than it was in the 1770s. We have every opportunity to make something of ourselves and then do what each generation before has continually done—make our own contribution. In the years leading up to the American Revolution, the original thirteen colonies had sought resolution with England. After finally deciding that their efforts were futile, this collection of colonies that had no real national identity came together for the one thing they had in common: a desire for independence. The odds against them were incredible, and yet they came together and paid a great price for liberty, both for themselves and for all who would follow. They saw the hope of something better, and many sensed that a great day in history had arrived.

In 1774, John Adams, the future second president of the United States, made the journey from his home in Quincy, Massachusetts, to Philadelphia, where he took his place as a delegate to the First Continental Congress. As he prepared to leave home, he despaired over the inexperience of his countrymen compared to the worldly accomplishments of the British. Adams himself had never traveled out of New England, and his only political experience was limited to a stint in the Massachusetts legislature that lasted less than a year. As he considered the work that was to come and the possibility of facing down the greatest power in the world, Adams wrote, "We have not men fit for the times. We are deficient in genius, education, in travel, fortune—in everything. I feel unutterable anxiety."[77]

Looking back through the lens of history, it's hard to imagine such words coming from a man who was part of a group of individuals who would come to be known as some of the greatest and brightest that ever lived. And yet in fact, his prognosis at that time was mostly accurate. The British Empire of the eighteenth century was the envy of the world. It had an envied military, a strong economy strengthened by colonies around the globe, and a population that was educated, well-traveled, and accomplished. The colonies of 1700s America were inhabited by people whose lives and viewpoints seldom saw anything beyond their own colony's borders, let alone the sophisticated capitals of Europe.

What was it that enabled these men and women of such deficiencies to accomplish such great feats? First, there was recognition of their shortcomings. They had no history of great military or worldly success to lull them into complacency. They realized their order was tall and they realized they had to do things differently to succeed. More importantly, they knew their cause was just and they relied on a higher Being, hoping that Being would also see their cause as just.

Second, these great individuals came together and seized what they saw as a special moment in the history of the world. Personal gain or ulterior motives had to come second to the common good of everyone. Those who pursued independence did so with the knowledge that traitors to the English Crown were hung. The motto "Live free or die" was not mere words. The selfish individual looking for self-aggrandizement would certainly not take such a risk. Somehow these colonists saw this moment as bigger than themselves, and their ardent desire to contribute to that moment drove their actions. After years of seeking to ease London's increasingly burdensome policies, they determined that independence, the point of last resort, was the only answer. Once this group of "deficient" men came to that conclusion, the die was cast. They saw what had to be done for them, their families, their countrymen, and the world. Their devotion to making this contribution enabled them to become "men fit for the times."

Through our history as a nation, we've learned that our country is also preserved at a price. Each succeeding generation of Americans has had to work to grow our nation and maintain our liberty while sacrificing for the common good of the nation. The early days of our republic were difficult, and progress came slowly. In today's world, emerging democracies can see what we have now through immediate exposure in the media and social networking. They see it and want it immediately without realizing that America's greatness isn't in possessions and lifestyle. It came from an inspired and sound set of principles and beliefs that created an environment where the bastion of freedom can reward everyone. It also required work, patience, sacrifice, and a commitment to the ideals that made it available. What the world sees now has been in the making for over two hundred years.

These ideals have endured and our liberty has held firm because our ancestors came together to preserve something greater than themselves time after time after time. The War of 1812, the Mexican War, the Civil War, financial panics of the late 1800s, the Spanish American War, World War I, the Great Depression, World War II, wars and conflicts in Korea and Vietnam, and civil rights movements have all tested the metal of the American people. Our heritage is rich and has a foundation that is far deeper than the world's despots can comprehend. It is not taken away nor given freely; it is earned by those who are willing to pay the price and kept by those who understand that they too must pay a price and contribute by passing along this heritage to the next generation.

When my Uncle Bert, a World War II hero, passed away, I was unprepared for the overwhelming emotions that came as I listened to the twenty-one-gun salute and the playing of "Taps" during his graveside service. With tears suddenly and uncontrollably streaming down my face, I couldn't speak a word. When he was drafted right after he graduated from tiny Central High School in rural central Utah, he left his home and everything that was safe and familiar and went to the South Pacific to preserve our liberty. He sat low in boats, gripped with fear, and then ran through the shallow waters of the Pacific with hundreds of American soldiers alongside him, trying to take a beachhead and hopefully an island. Once at the beach he frantically crawled through the sand, hoping to reach a foxhole while gunfire whizzed all around him. As a medic, he was shot while tending to other wounded soldiers. As "Taps" played at his funeral, I saw my uncle as the defender of freedom he was, a young man far away from home, fighting for me, a nephew he hadn't yet met. These contributions made by so many before us have provided and preserved an environment of freedom, opportunity, education, innovation, medicine, and luxury that are the envy of the world. Too many of us have no concept of the struggles that so many throughout the world endure.

This message of contribution, of preserving the good and leaving it better for the next generation, is vital to our existence. In it we find the recipe for service, doing good, and lifting those whose hands fall down. It's always been in those defining moments of greatest difficulty that mankind has risen to the occasion and to the God-like potential that is in each of us.

When the Constitutional Convention closed in Philadelphia in 1787, Dr. Benjamin Franklin, one of those great founders of America, gave one last reminder to each generation of our obligation to contribute, to remember the histories of sacrifice, and maintain what we've been given. As Franklin walked down the steps of Independence Hall on the final day, a group approached him and asked, "Well Doctor, what have we got, a republic or a monarchy?" Franklin replied, "A republic, if you can keep it."[78]

What a powerful message. My fellow fathers, this is our call to action. Our ancestors have preserved this republic for more than 230 years, and their cause of contribution must be ours as well. Spend time with your children; teach them about what is good and right about our communities. And remember, your cause as fathers is also just, and you can rely on the same higher power to help you achieve success. While our challenges may not be on a battlefield, we need to answer the call to defend truth, freedom, and goodness. Let us stand up and fulfill our civic, religious, and personal duties to make our piece of the world a little better. And as we do this collectively as the world's fraternity of fathers, we will show our children what it means to contribute and preserve what is right and what is good.

― 13 ―

The Windermere

Lessons on Discipleship

"You can only hit the snooze button so many times."

On February 22, 1854, a British sailing vessel called the *Windermere* weighed anchor, opened its sails, and departed from the crowded Port of Liverpool on England's central west coast. The Liverpool of the mid-1800s had long been a major hub for people and goods going to foreign lands, and its port and warehouses were cutting edge for the times. With its neo-classical domed customhouse and stately brick warehouses, the port was also home to the new, state-of-the-art Albert Dock (now called Royal Albert Dock). Completed only eight years prior, it was the first structure in Great Britain to be built of cast iron, brick, and stone. Built around a basin, the dock complex and its noncombustible warehouse system enabled ships to enter and load and unload cargo directly at the warehouses, an innovative system of the era that cut loading times in half.[79]

Among those listed in the *Windermere*'s logbook for the voyage that day was a thirty-four-year-old leather tanner named Stephen Williams. Issued ticket number 101, Stephen was joined by his pregnant twenty-seven-year-old wife, Emma Jane, and their four children ranging from ages eleven years to eighteen months. A few years previously while living in Bristol, England, their lives had taken a dramatic turn when they met missionaries and were baptized into The Church of Jesus Christ of Latter-day Saints. This change in their lives resulted in abuse, ridicule, rejection, and job loss. Abandoned by family and friends and unable to find work, Stephen and Emma Jane sold all they had, borrowed from the Perpetual Emigration Fund, and prepared to sail for Zion.

Under cold, late-winter skies, Stephen and his family arrived at the already crowded Port of Liverpool early on the morning of the 22nd. Navigating the legion of horse-drawn carriages, they walked past gangplank after gangplank brimming with chests and bags waiting to be loaded. Simultaneously, they kept a lookout for the endless gauntlet of thieves known as "runners" who were eagerly scouting luggage to steal and pockets to pick. Amid the din of goods being loaded onto ships, the clamor of excited passengers saying goodbye, and the bustle of agents taking care of last-minute business, Stephen finally found their company leader, who led his family to their loading zone. In addition to its fame as a center for worldwide transportation, this great port was also the major hub for members of The Church of Jesus Christ of Latter-day Saints immigrating to America, and on this February Wednesday, the *Windermere* would depart with 460 of them.

With the hopeful on board singing hymns of praise, the tall ship finally eased out into the River Mersey and gradually headed north and slightly west. Reaching the mouth of the river, the *Windermere* was hurled into the rough Irish Sea, which howled with strong winds and crashing waves, blowing the ship off course. With the ship drifting north, the struggling crew finally wrestled control and veered it toward the west. Some sixty miles later at around 11:00 p.m. and with the darkness-shrouded hills of Dublin lying another sixty or so miles to the west, the *Windermere* rounded the Welch Island of Anglesey and passed the treacherous point of Holyhead, a literal ship's graveyard on many dark, stormy nights. With gale-force winds still ripping at the ship's massive sails, anxious seasick passengers huddled below deck as the creaking, groaning *Windermere* veered south and surged onward against the waves into the black night. Hours later, they would pass through St. George's Channel into the Celtic Sea and then, finally, into the vast Atlantic Ocean beyond.

Bound for New Orleans, Louisiana, the weary travelers aboard the *Windermere* still had much to endure on the long journey ahead of them. They encountered weeks of contrary winds and fierce storms, endured an outbreak of smallpox, saw a fire break out under the cooking galley, and witnessed six marriages, six births, and ten deaths. Finally, after five weeks, a favorable wind set in, and the *Windermere* sailed one thousand miles in four days. After eight-and-a-half long weeks at sea, they finally arrived in New Orleans on April 23, 1854.[80]

Four days after arriving in New Orleans, Stephen and Emma Jane loaded their family onto a steam-powered ship that made its way up the Mississippi River to St. Louis. From there, their journey took them west to Kansas City and then north where they joined a company of Saints headed toward the Salt Lake Valley.

Just over seven months after their departure from Liverpool, Stephen and Emma Jane Williams arrived in Salt Lake City on September 30, 1854. Along the way, they buried their eighteen-month-old son and welcomed a new baby boy, born in a covered wagon just west of Council Bluffs, Iowa. Within three years of their arrival to the Salt Lake Valley, the family would be called to move to central Utah to help settle the new town of Ephraim. Ultimately, Stephen and Emma Jane would have a total of twelve children, ten of whom would grow to adulthood. As committed disciples of Christ, Stephen and Emma Jane raised their family in an atmosphere of love, faith, and sacrifice. Stephen's was a hope and faith that his sacrifices, hardships, and life's effort to build his family would leave a legacy of building and lifting others to God.

I think often of the contributions of this father, my great-great-grandfather, who left everything that was comfortable and everyone he knew to follow his faith and lead his family on the pathway directed by God. Like you, so much of who I am and what I've become have been molded by the sacrifices and examples of ancestors who gave up so much. We all have the common thread of having ancestors who sacrificed to benefit their posterity. When we dig into the family well, we find a reservoir of stories we can build on. Further, as we think over the course of our lives, we come to realize we've had our fair share of challenges. Thus, our stories are added to those from the past and our own posterity is blessed by them. As our children persevere through the challenges that will come, the experiences of those who went before and endured become part of the foundation that offers pride during times of plenty and strength during times of scarcity. While some may have deeper foundations than others, each one of us has a foundation based upon the one Christ Himself built for us. The greatest legacy we can leave our children is the continuation of that legacy, which, with our experiences added, becomes a living, never-ending blueprint.

Among Stephen's numerous grandchildren was my grandfather, Neldon Williams. Born on August 1, 1900, my grandpa was his own type of Renaissance man. When his father died, he dropped out of school at the age of fourteen to become a coal miner. Later, after a broken leg forced him out of the depths of the caverns, he bought a pickup truck, painted "Williams Roofing" on the door, and went into business. Along the way, he owned a hot dog shop, danced himself into oblivion, and played semi-pro baseball, a wizard on both sides of the ball. Among the many things he did, one talent that stood out was his master craftsmanship.

My grandfather, a man who built things to last, would be appalled by today's put-it-together-yourself, it-looks-like-wood bookshelves. The many items he built from wood were solid, and the proof was in the pudding. When his hand-built wooden camper blew off his truck one day in the mid-1950s as he drove full speed down the highway, all he had to do was turn around and get some help from other motorists to heft his unscathed masterpiece back on the truck. Further evidence was in the three-piece bedroom set he built for my mom and dad. Dropped from an airplane, this hulking bedroom suite could've taken out an entire village. The great thing about my grandpa was that the way in which he built things mirrored the way he built his family. He kept them close, taught them to love, and built a solid family foundation where love and faith would last.

President David O. McKay once stated that in our day of judgment, the Savior will ask for an accounting of our "earthly responsibilities." Said President McKay,

> First, He will request an accountability report about your relationship with your wife. Have you actively been engaged in making her happy and ensuring that her needs have been met as an individual?
>
> Second, He will want an accountability report about each of your children individually. He will not attempt to have this for simply a family stewardship but will request information about your relationship to each and every child.
>
> Third, He will want to know what you personally have done with the talents you were given in the pre-existence.
>
> Fourth, He will want a summary of your activity in your church assignments. He will not be necessarily interested in what assignments you have had, for in his eyes the home teacher and a mission president are probably equals, but He will request a summary of how you have been of service to your fellowmen in your Church assignments.
>
> Fifth, He will have no interest in how you earned your living, but if you were honest in all your dealings.

Sixth, He will ask for an accountability on what you have done to contribute in a positive manner to your community, state, country, and the world.[81]

It will be our character—honesty, charity, civility, and integrity—that will matter and not wealth or position. Did we indeed develop the characteristics of God and seek to become like Him? These will be the hallmarks of the great and noble ones of eternity.

If these are the things that matter to our Heavenly Father, it then becomes vital to our children's salvation that we exert every effort to teach them these things so they may be prepared for the interview that is to come for them. Each of us must, at some point in our lives, decide who we'll follow. This choice manifests itself in ways that are both bold and subtle, and often it's the subtleties that can trip us up the most. Options in entertainment and recreation, our career paths, acquiring possessions, or even the difficulty of accepting change can cause us to lose our focus on the better part of discipleship.

An example from early Church history is a reminder of the Lord's desire that we follow Him and do so with urgency. In 1838, the Lord directed Joseph Smith to build up Far West, Missouri, and among those called to go was a group called the Kirtland Company. When the party left Kirtland that summer, only half heeded the call. Among the no-shows were William Marks and Newell K. Whitney, Kirtland's bishop who presided over the Church's distribution of goods.[82]

Unhappy because those who didn't come were too concerned about sacrificing temporal things, the Lord chastised them in Doctrine and Covenants 117. In doing so He referenced Nicolas from the New Testament, a man who, like Bishop Whitney, was charged with the distribution of goods for the Church in Jerusalem. Some believed that Nicolas left the Church with followers who were referred to as Nicolaitans.[83] In Doctrine and Covenants 117:11, the Lord said, "Let my servant Newell

K. Whitney be ashamed of the Nicolaitane band and of all their secret abominations." The Lord was candid in His reminder that a halfway effort is no effort at all. Elder Neal A. Maxwell, former member of the Quorum of the Twelve Apostles of The Church of Jesus Christ of Latter-day Saints, referred to this group of people within the Church when he spoke of those who seek a "mansion in heaven but desire to keep a cottage in the world."[84]

As we teach our children to lift themselves so they can see God, we help them understand that following the world and its ideas of acceptable behavior will afford them a wide array of philosophies. They'll discover that the gradual and continual erosion of society's moral compass has created an atmosphere where incivility, immorality, cunning, and deceit thrive. This crippling hit parade delights the adversary, whose influence is felt strongly in a world where, as Elder Gerrit W. Gong of the Quorum of the Twelve Apostles states, "the sacred is made common and the holy is made profane."[85]

One of the most humbling experiences of my life came at a time when, wanting to draw closer to the Lord, I prayed and asked Him to take the world out of me. Less than three months later, I was looking out of a fourth-floor hospital window as an ambulance whisked my newborn son to Primary Children's Hospital. My worry of how my recent job loss would enable me to pay for all the medical expenses was substantially overshadowed by the realization that my baby boy might not survive the night. A little over a year later, with a new job and a healthy one-year-old in tow, I stood with a friend on a downtown Salt Lake City street corner discussing trials. When he asked me if I felt the Lord was efficient, I told him of my experience to offer proof. However difficult it may be, this process of having the world taken out of us is required for our journey back to God.

In Exodus chapter 17, Moses led the children of Israel to a new location with no water. Thirsty, stressed, and forgetful of the many miracles

God had performed on their behalf, the Israelites found themselves murmuring and asking the question we all ask ourselves at times: "Is the Lord among us, or not?" (Exodus 17:7). Moses was then instructed to smite a rock. Upon his doing so, water gushed from the rock, giving the Israelites another miracle and the relief they needed. Then, as he is wont to do at times of our weakness, the adversary came calling. The next verse reads, "And then came Amalek and fought with Israel in Rephidim" (Exodus 17:8). Amalek, the grandson of Esau, led a nomadic tribe that became known as Amalek, or the Amalekites. Inhabiting the land south of Canaan, this enemy of Israel took every opportunity to attack, and with Israel floundering in a weakened spiritual state, the adversary moved upon the Amalekites, who went straight into battle mode.

With this development, Moses instructed Joshua to lead the Israelites while Moses stood and watched from a hill. When Moses' hands were raised, Israel gained strength, but when he tired and lowered them, Israel began to succumb to the enemy. Israel ultimately prevailed when those who were with Moses assisted him and held his arms up. Then came the statement from the Lord in verses 14–16: "And the Lord said unto Moses, Write this for a memorial in a book, and rehearse it in the ears of Joshua: for I will utterly put out the remembrance of Amalek from under heaven. And Moses built an altar, and called the name of it Jehovah-nissi: for he said, Because the Lord hath sworn that the Lord will have war with Amalek from generation to generation."

The message of this Old Testament battle is surely a lesson to live by. First, when we complain and question whether God is with us, doesn't the adversary come quickly, taking advantage of our weakest moments? Second, when we can see God or those He has called to lead and help us, we're given the strength to win our battles with the adversary. When we can't, that strength isn't there. Lastly, in comparing Amalek to the world, the Lord teaches us that the battle against Amalek, or the world, will rage from generation to generation. In words that can't be misunderstood, He lets us know He "will utterly put out the remembrance" of the world. In tragic contrast, the world has put aside the things of God. Our children and grandchildren must know that the Lord has established the path, along with its qualifying behaviors, that will lead them back to God. And while this covenant path will never be in vogue in a society that views it as old-fashioned, it is the only true source of peace and happiness.

The fifth chapter of Alma is a powerful reminder of what life on earth is all about. This life is a preparatory period for each of us to come to know God and do all we can to become like Him. In verses 14–15 and 19, Alma teaches,

> And now behold, I ask of you, my brethren of the church, have ye spiritually been born of God? Have ye received his image in your countenances? Have ye experienced this mighty change in your hearts? Do ye exercise faith in the redemption of him who created you? Do you look forward with an eye of faith, and view this mortal body raised in immortality, and this corruption raised in incorruption, to stand before God to be judged according to the deeds which have been done in the mortal body? I say unto you, can ye look up to God at that day with a pure heart and clean hands? I say unto you, can you look up, having the image of God engraven upon your countenances?

Alma then provides insight as to what it means to have the image of God "engraven upon" us. We must assess our thoughts and actions by asking ourselves the questions in this chapter: Have we yielded ourselves to the adversary or have we not? Have we stripped ourselves of pride, of envy, of vanity? Have we been charitable toward others, and are we humble and blameless, that we may stand before God with our garments washed white and clean? Our vigilant attention to our coming unto Christ is what enables this mighty change of heart. Further, this vigil isn't an isolated occurrence;

it's a daily process. All of this requires great humility, for certainly it will be those without guile, or in other words, those who are pure, who will be able to come unto Him. Then we'll be among those who will bring forth good fruit and be called by name by our Shepherd. And having learned the sound of his voice, we will hear Him.

Imagine the deep sorrows and numerous problems that would be alleviated if fathers around the world understood and accepted this accountability. Imagine how much infidelity, abuse, and neglect could be avoided—spiritually catastrophic events that come with such high-cost premiums. At a time when I was traveling a great deal, my wife reminded me as I sat in a Denver, Colorado, hotel room of my responsibilities when she said, "Remember, we're counting on you." With their husband and father alone and away, my wonderful little family at home was counting on my faithfulness and integrity. JoAnn's comment was a gentle reminder that they believed in me and trusted me to do only those things that would enable continued blessings for our family—blessings predicated upon obedience (see Doctrine and Covenants 130:20–21). As I thought of my wife and children, I realized what a great privilege it was to be counted on.

It also reminded me of the power of our thoughts as well as our actions. Elder Melvin J. Ballard, a member of the Quorum of the Twelve Apostles for The Church of Jesus Christ of Latter-day Saints from 1919 through 1939, used his last words in mortality to teach a great lesson on the power of our thoughts. During a 1983 address given at Brigham Young University, his grandson, President M. Russell Ballard, then of the Seventy, said "Grandfather pushed himself up in bed, looked into his hospital room as though he were addressing a congregation or a group, and said clearly, "And above all else, brethren, let us think straight."[86] What great strength and insight we can gain from those words from an Apostle.

In Matthew 25, the Lord related the parable of the ten virgins. None of the ten knew when the bridegroom would come; however, five were ready with oil in their lamps while the other five "slumbered and slept" (Matthew 25:5). Suddenly there was a cry: "Behold, the bridegroom cometh; go ye out to meet him" (Matthew 25:6). While the five who already had their oil were ready, the five who slumbered were not. Caught by surprise, they sought to borrow from the five wise virgins; however, upon finding the oil couldn't be borrowed, they were shut out from the marriage.

We can pursue so many worthy endeavors in this life. However, this parable reminds us of the endeavor that everything else pales in comparison to—that of making sure our families are prepared to meet the bridegroom. So often we can err by thinking the five unprepared virgins were women of wickedness or who didn't believe. But these five virgins were much like the five who had oil; they knew the bridegroom was coming and were awaiting the marriage. Unfortunately, somewhere along the way, they'd allowed complacency to enter their lives. Their slumbering and sleeping could well represent a lack of spiritual engagement or the lie of procrastination that tells us we still have plenty of time. We too know the Lord will come soon; however, do we keep oil in our lamps? Do we remain steadfast, and do we push ourselves and our families to the Lord? Do we have a sense of urgency, and do we make sure no earthly endeavor overrides our endeavors to follow the only One who can save us? When the foolish virgins tried to borrow, they didn't realize that in the day of His coming, the days for preparation had ended. They couldn't move forward on borrowed covenants.

When I consider the importance of being prepared, I realize these last days call for the greatest leadership the world has ever seen. And while our time requires great leadership in all realms, perhaps the most important, yet often overlooked, is the place where it all begins and what will be most valued in the eternities—the family. The calling of a father is divine, and it must be our top priority along with our role as husbands. In the fight against the adversary, fathers must lead with trust and create an environment of love and security. We must also remember that our example is the best remedy for any problem. On more than one occasion, one of my children has watched me and then exclaimed, "Dad, when you do that, I do that." Like millions of fathers before me, I wondered what I had just done.

In today's world, there's no room for complacency or procrastination. Now is a time for urgency. The time for men of God to rise up is today. It requires patience, consistency, and a focus on what matters most. It requires prayer, study, and faith so we can ever move upward. And it requires love, devotion, and learning. When it comes to standing up and realizing our potential, I'm reminded of the oft-stated phrase "You can only hit the snooze button so many times." How true that is. It pertains to how quickly our children grow up, how fast our lives go by, and how unknown the moment is when it will be our time to meet God. The time is now to love, cherish, and bless our wives and children.

The Lord's hope for and calling to us are to covenant with Him—to release our nets and follow Him. That following is not only in the saying; it's in the doing, the living, and the letting go of the world. And for those who choose to do so, the ensuing blessings of true peace and joy, as well as God's promises, provide a sense of happiness and greatness beyond our comprehension. Indeed, the gospel is the "good news" to Heavenly Father's children. If the choice is to choose God or the world, why is the decision so difficult? During the Savior's ministry when many of His disciples "went back, and walked no more with him" (John 6:66), the Lord said to His twelve disciples in John 6:67, "Will ye also go away?" Peter's response was, in my mind, one of the greatest realizations in the history of mankind. In verse 68, Peter answered, "Lord, to whom shall we go? thou hast the words of eternal life." This profound message will always bring peace and hope to us and our families.

How then do we leave our nets and follow Him? It is done as Elder Maxwell stated—through daily effort. It is done through prayer, fasting, and study. It is done as Alma confessed—through "a mighty change of heart." We must desire to change and be willing to do whatever is necessary to elevate our thinking, our doing, our speaking, and our whole plane of living. Through these efforts, our love for Him grows, we become more like Him, and our perspective becomes more aligned with His. Then we can be called men and women of God. Our minds are clear, and we can view our lives within the quiet realms of the Spirit as the noise of the world passes by. This perspective is what I refer to as the cadence of God. And it's what brings to my mind Peter's answer to the Savior: "Lord, to whom shall we go?"

When we know to whom we should go, we can become "steadfast and immovable" (Mosiah 5:15). Then we can positively impact lives, our families, and the world. Our aim as fathers should be to lead our children through the ebbs and flows of mortality, to bless them, to build them, and to help them become disciples of Christ. With that discipleship comes the self-discipline that enables control of thoughts and appetites. Our role as fathers and disciples is not to give our children everything. Our role is to love them, teach them, and help them come to know God so they can get back to Him. Then *He* can give them everything. We should never forget that these children we love so dearly belonged to our Heavenly Father first. As we build upon the foundation He and His Son provided and build upon the strengths and abilities He sent our children with, we work toward our Father's greatest aspiration for His children and ours—the immortality and eternal life of each one.

Many years ago, my carpenter grandfather purchased a set of carpentry books entitled *Audels Carpenters and Builders Guide* by Franklin D. Graham. The first page of each guidebook includes a quote from John Ruskin, a nineteenth-century artist, writer, social thinker, and philanthropist. Ruskin's quote on carpentry is one of the most accurate reflections on building I've ever seen. While written to the craftsman, it's a meaningful message to anyone who builds anything in any form.

> When we build, let us think that we build forever. Let it not be for present delight nor for present use alone. Let it be such work as our descendents will thank us for; and let us think, as we lay stone on stone, that a time is to come when those stones will be held sacred because our hands have touched them, and that men will say, as they look upon the labor and wrought substance of them, See! This our father did for us.[87]

In these words are reminders of the hands of our Heavenly Father who, in great glory, created the plan of salvation and directed the creation of this earth for us to stand on. In its words I see the hands of my many grandfathers who built a legacy for me to stand on as well as the hands of my father who built a home and a life for me to stand on—one of love, faith, priorities, and discipleship. I see these words come to life each morning when the sun rises, and I realize what God has created for me. I see them each time I read of the hardships of my ancestors and understand what they sacrificed for me. Ruskin's words are now my blueprint for the legacy I wish to build for my children. With that in mind, I encourage you to consider the legacy you hope to leave for your children and then expend every effort to achieve it.

And so, to the men of the world, let us all go on in the great and noble causes of fatherhood and discipleship, leading out and building stone upon stone so our children will know who to turn to, who to follow, and how to return to the Father who created them. The need for exactness, the need for honor, and the need for character have never been greater. Let us do as John Ruskin penned and build our children for the eternities.

Notes

James E. Faust, "Them That Honour Me Will I Honour," *Ensign* (The Church of Jesus Christ of Latter-day Saints, Salt Lake City, May 2001), 47–49.

1. Mark Wahlberg, *People Magazine Peoplebabies*, January 27, 2011.
2. Thomas S. Monson, "Be Strong and of a Good Courage," *Ensign*, April 2014, 69.
3. See "Famous Quotes by Vince Lombardi," vincelombardi.com/quotes, accessed February 11, 2022, www.vincelombardi.com/quotes.
4. Joseph Fielding Smith ed., *Teachings of the Prophet Joseph Smith* (Salt Lake City: Deseret Book, 1938), 159.
5. Ezra Taft Benson, "What I Hope You Will Teach Your Children about the Temple," *Ensign*, August 1985, 8.
6. See "Patriarch." Merriam-Webster.com Dictionary, Merriam-Webster, accessed April 7, 2022, merriam-webster.com/dictionary/patriarch.
7. See "Pater." Merriam-Webster.com Dictionary, Merriam-Webster, accessed April 7, 2022, merriam-webster.com/dictionary/pater.
8. David McCullough, *Truman* (New York: Simon & Schuster, 1992), 927.
9. Dale G. Renlund, "Unwavering Commitment to Jesus Christ," *Ensign*, November 2019, 22.
10. Henry B. Eyring, "O Remember, Remember," *Ensign*, November 2007, 66.

11. Howard W. Hunter, *The Teachings of Howard W. Hunter* (Salt Lake City: Deseret Book, 1997), 74.
12. Joseph B. Wirthlin, "Finding a Safe Harbor," *Ensign*, May 2000, 66.
13. Dale G. Renlund, "Unwavering Commitment to Jesus Christ," *Ensign*, November 2019), 22.
14. Elaine Dalton, "Love Her Mother," *Ensign*, November 2011, 77.
15. J. Devn Cornish, "The Privilege of Prayer," *Ensign*, November 2011, 101.
16. The Quorum of the Twelve Apostles, Produced and Written by Christopher S. Clark and Patrick H. Parker, "Earthly Father, Heavenly Father," *The Mormon Channel* (Brigham Young University Motion Picture Studios, Provo, 2013), Used with permission.
17. See "Poplar Grove Neighborhood," Salt Lake City Council District 2, accessed on October 21, 2022, slc.gov/district2/tour-district-2/poplar-grove/.
18. Thomas S. Monson, "Hallmarks of a Happy Home," *Ensign*, November 1988.
19. See "Quotes Falsely Attributed to Winston Churchill," International Churchill Society, accessed October 12, 2022, winstonchurchill.org/resources/quotes/quotes-falsely-attributed/.
20. Willard Sterne Randall, *Thomas Jefferson: A Life* (New York: New York, 1993), 355, 356.
21. Willard Sterne Randall, *Thomas Jefferson: A Life* (New York: Henry Holt and Company, 1993), 356, 370.
22. See Melvin L. Bashore & Scott Crump, *Riverton: The Story of a Utah Country Town* (Salt Lake City: Publishers Press, 1994), 116.
23. Michelle D. Craig, "Spiritual Capacity," *Ensign*, November 2019, 19.
24. Michelle D. Craig, "Spiritual Capacity," *Ensign*, November 2019, 19.
25. See Tom Verducci, "Game Changer: How Carlton Fisk's Home Run Altered Baseball and TV," *Sports Illustrated*, October 26, 2015, 106.

26. See "Paul Harvey Quotations," quotetab.com., accessed October 12, 2022, quotetab.com/quotes/by-paul-harvey.
27. See Phil Alden Robinson, *Field of Dreams* (Universal Studios, 1989), adapted from *Shoeless Joe*, W.P. Kinsella (Houghton Mifflin Harcourt, Boston, 1982).
28. Grantland Rice, *Alumnus Football*, last two lines, from *"Only the Brave and Other Poems"* (New York: A.S. Barnes and Co., 1941) 144.
29. See "Being Wise in Time," Chronicles of America, accessed February 11, 2022, chroniclesofamerica.com/theodore-roosevelt/being_wise_in_time.
30. Thomas S. Monson, "Finding Joy in the Journey," *Ensign*, November 2008, 84.
31. See Produced and Written by Christopher S. Clark and Patrick H. Parker, "Earthly Father, Heavenly Father," *The Mormon Channel* (Brigham Young University Motion Picture Studios, Provo, 2013), Used with permission.
32. See Produced and Written by Christopher S. Clark and Patrick H. Parker, "Earthly Father, Heavenly Father," *The Mormon Channel* (Brigham Young University Motion Picture Studios, Provo, 2013), used with permission.
33. See *Historic Sites and Structures of Hancock County, Illinois*, The Church of Jesus Christ of Latter-day Saints, Church History Library, call number 977.3 H6723 1979.
34. See "The Mississippi River and Expansion of America," accessed October 11, 2022, legendsofamerica.com/ah-mississippiriver/.
35. See "Louisiana Purchase" Office of the Historian, U.S. Department of State, accessed February 11, 2022, history.state.gov/milestones/1801-1829/louisiana-purchase.
36. See "Revelation, 20 July 1831 [D&C 57]," The Joseph Smith Papers, vol.1, 93, josephsmithpapers.org/paper-summary/revelation-20-july-1831-dc-57/1.

37. See "Missouri Compromise," History, accessed on October 20, 2022, history.com/topics/abolitionist-movement/missouri-compromise; "Missouri officially enters the United States," Missouri Courts, accessed on October 20, 2022, courts.mo.gov/page.jsp?id=174522#:~:text=The%20Missouri%20territorial%20legislature%20approved,24th%20state%20in%20the%20union.
38. See "Far West," The Church of Jesus Christ of latter-day Saints, accessed on October 20, 2022, churchofjesuschrist.org/study/history/topics/far-west?lang=eng.
39. See "Extermination Order," The Church of Jesus Christ of Latter-day Saints, accessed October 20, 2022, churchofjesuschrist.org/study/history/topics/extermination-order?lang=eng.
40. See "Haun's Mill Massacre" The Church of Jesus Christ of Latter-day Saints, accessed October 11, 2022, churchofjesuschrist.org/study/history/topics/hawns-mill-massacre.
41. See "Liberty Jail," The Church of Jesus Christ of Latter-day Saints, accessed October 11, 2022, www.churchofjesuschrist.org/study/history/topics/liberty-jail?lang=eng.
42. See ibid.
43. T. H. Breen, *George Washington's Journey* (New York: Simon & Schuster, 2016), 83–109.
44. See "Liberty Jail," The Church of Jesus Christ of Latter-day Saints, accessed October 11, 2022, churchofjesuschrist.org/study/history/topics/liberty-jail?lang=eng.
45. See Susan Easton Black, "How Large Was the Population of Nauvoo?" *BYU Studies*, 1995, byustudies.byu.edu/article/how-large-was-the-population-of-nauvoo/.
46. See Kyle M. Rollins, Richard D. Smith, M. Brett Borup, E. James Nelson, "Transforming Swampland into Nauvoo, the City Beautiful A Civil Engineering Perspective" *BYU Studies*, accessed on October 20, 2022, byustudies.byu.edu/article/transforming-

swampland-into-nauvoo-the-city-beautiful-a-civil-engineering-perspective/.
47. See Directed and Produced by Frank Capra, Screenplay by Frances Goodrich, Albert Hacking, Frank Capra, and Jo Swerling, *It's a Wonderful Life*, based on *The Greatest Gift* by Philip Van Doren Stern (RKO Pictures, 1946).
48. See Tom Brokaw, *The Greatest Generation* (New York: Penguin Random House, 2004).
49. See "Attack on Pearl Harbor—1941," accessed February 11, 2022, World War II History from Atomic Heritage Foundation, June 18, 2014; "Pearl Harbor Attack," accessed February 11, 2022, Japanese–United States History from The Editors of Encyclopedia Britannica, June 25, 2019.
50. Gordon B. Hinckley, "Stand True and Faithful," *Ensign*, May 1996, 93.
51. See Sean Covey, *The 7 Habits of Highly Effective Teens* (New York: Simon & Schuster, 1998, 2014 by Franklin Covey Co.), 16.
52. See Jennifer K. Nii, "100 years of Snappy Service—Diner thrives at new home in Sandy," *Deseret News*, Aug 28, 2002.
53. David A. Bednar, *Receiving, Recognizing, and Responding to the Promptings of the Holy Ghost* (Ricks College Devotional, Aug 31, 1999).
54. Lynne Cheney, *James Madison: A Life Reconsidered* (New York: Viking, 2014), 2, 18, 23–33.
55. See Roger Cormier, "20 Memorable Facts About the Miracle on Ice," *Mental Floss*, February 20, 2015, accessed on October 22, 2022, mentalfloss.com/article/61728/20-things-you-might-not-know-about-miracle-ice.
56. See Joe Posnanski, "Memories of the Miracle on Ice," NBC Sports, February 14, 2014, accessed on October 22, 2022, olympics.nbcsports.com/2014/02/14/memories-of-the-miracle-on-ice/.
57. See Zachary D. Rymer, "They're Going Crazy: The Top Ten In-The-Moment Calls Ever Made" (The Bleacher Report, Aug 15, 2010).

58. Sean Gregory, "Why Muhammad Ali Matters to Everyone," *Time Magazine*, June 4, 2016, accessed on October 22, 2022, time.com/3646214/muhammad-ali-dead-obituary/.

59. Peter Angelo Simon, *Muhammad Ali away from the spotlight at Fighter's Heaven,* The Telegraph, June 4, 2016.

60. Brad Rock, "Looking Back at the Jazz", *Deseret News*, October 30, 1990.

61. See Joe Posnanski, "Memories of the Miracle on Ice," NBC Sports, February 14, 2014, accessed on October 22, 2022, olympics.nbcsports.com/2014/02/14/memories-of-the-miracle-on-ice/.

62. David Nasaw, *Andrew Carnegie* (New York: The Penguin Press, 2006), 34, 35.

63. David Nasaw, *Andrew Carnegie* (New York: The Penguin Press, 2006), 35.

64. David Nasaw, *Andrew Carnegie* (New York: The Penguin Press, 2006), 35.

65. Theodore Roosevelt, *The Key to Success in Life* (New York: Federated Publishing Company, 1916).

66. Jolene Brown, Conference Address to the Idaho Bankers Association, February 2008, Used with permission.

67. Ronald C. White, Jr., *A. Lincoln* (New York: Random House, 2009), 113.

68. Eric Zorn, "Without Failure, Jordan Would Be False Idol," *Chicago Tribune*, May 19, 1997.

69. Compiled by Peggy Anderson, *Great Quotes from Great Leaders* (Franklin Lakes, NJ: Career Press, 1997), 35.

70. Jack Canfield, *The Success Principles* (New York: Harper Collins, 2005), 11.

71. Nathan Miller, *Theodore Roosevelt: A Life* (New York: William Morrow and Company, 1992), 507.

72. See "Ellis Island History," The Statue of Liberty—Ellis Island Foundation, accessed February 11, 2022, statueofliberty.org; "The Immigrant Journey," Ellis Island National Monument, accessed February 11, 2022, ohranger.com.

73. See Carrie A. Moore & James Greaves, "Small loans making a huge difference: Microcredit milestone is celebrated in S.L," *Deseret News*, October 31, 2005.

74. Mentors International (Draper, UT, Dec 2019), used with permission.

75. See Carrie A. Moore & James Greaves, "Small loans making a huge difference: Microcredit milestone is celebrated in S.L," *Deseret News*, October 31, 2005.

76. See Directed by Michael Hoffman, Produced by Marc Abraham, Andrew S. Karsch, Michael O'Neill, Screenplay by Neil Tolkin, *The Emperor's Club* based on *The Palace Thief* by Ethan Canin (Universal Pictures, 2002).

77. David McCullough, *John Adams* (New York: Simon & Schuster, 2001), 23.

78. Richard R. Beeman, Ph.D., *Perspectives on the Constitution: A Republic, If You Can Keep It* (National Constitution Center, Philadelphia).

79. See "History—Royal Albert Dock Liverpool," accessed February 11, 2022, albertdock.com and "Custom House, Liverpool, UK 1836–1948," accesses February 11, 2022, stolenhistory.org.

80. Sources include the following: *Stephen Williams and His Descendants*, Compiled by Clara Williams Woodfield, (Salt Lake City, 1978), 1–4; *The Voyage of the Ship Windermere*, H. Clay Gorton, Condensed from W.W. Burton's Account (March 23, 1944).

81. See "Understandings of the Heart," Robert D. Hales, BYU Speeches, accessed October 12, 2022, speeches.byu.edu/talks/robert-d-hales/understandings-heart/.

82. *Doctrine & Covenants Student Manual* (The Church of Jesus Christ of Latter-day Saints, Salt Lake City, 2002), 288–290.
83. See ibid.
84. Cory H. Maxwell ed., *The Neal A. Maxwell Quote Book* (Salt Lake City: Bookcraft, 1997), 25.
85. Gerrit W. Gong, "Room in the Inn," *Liahona*, May 2021, 24.
86. See "Let Us Think Straight," M. Russell Ballard, BYU Speeches, accessed October 12, 2022, speeches.byu.edu/talks/m-russell-ballard/let-us-think-straight/.
87. Frank D. Graham, *Audels Carpenters and Builders Guide* (New York City: Theo. Audel & Company, 1923, 1939, reprinted 1945), 1.

Note to the Reader

Thank you for accompanying me through some of what I feel are life's greatest lessons on fatherhood. Though often overwhelming and challenging, fatherhood truly is wonderfully worthwhile and fulfilling. It is my hope that you enjoy your journey and add your own lessons to your book of life.

For fathers and father figures: Please join me on my website, authorpauldwilliams.com, where you can read my blog, exchange ideas, and share traditions with fathers and father figures of all ages and from all walks of life.

And if you have enjoyed this book, please leave a review wherever fine books are sold.

Thank you, and "Let us all go on in the great and noble causes of fatherhood."

About the Author

Paul Williams has enjoyed his work in the banking industry for a number of years, but his real passion lies in his roles as a husband and father. A lifelong citizen of what he calls the most beautiful place in the world—Utah—he and his wife, JoAnn, are the proud, happy parents of seven wonderful children—three boys, three girls, and the final boy, whom Paul refers to as their "swing vote."

Paul was raised in a truly unique family that was extremely close. Uncles and neighbors doubled as father figures, and his dad, Duane, balanced extensive career and volunteer work while prioritizing his role as a father. Over the years, Paul has served as a father figure to nieces, nephews, neighbors, and, of course, his own children. Among his many diverse experiences and responsibilities, he finds his greatest joy in his family.